SEARCHING FOR TREASURE:

A GUIDE TO WISDOM AND CHARACTER DEVELOPMENT

By

Marty Elwell

Illustrated

By

Steve Rose

THE FAMILY LEARNING SERIES

NOBLE PUBLISHING ASSOCIATES

GRESHAM, OREGON

Noble Publishing Associates

Noble Publishing Associates, the publishing arm of Christian Life Workshops, is an association of Christian authors dedicated to serving God and assisting one another in the production, promotion, and distribution of audio, video, and print publications. For instructions on how you may participate in our association, or for information about our complete line of materials, write to:

Noble Publishing Associates
P.O. Box 2250
Gresham, Oregon 97030

or call (503) 667-3942.

All Scripture quotations, unless indicated are taken from the Holy Bible: New International Version, © 1973, 1978, 1984 by International Bible Society. Used by permission of Zondervan Publishing House. All rights reserved. The "NIV" and "New International Version" trademarks are registered in the United States Patent and Trademark Office by International Bible Society. Use of either trademark requires the permission of International Bible Society.

Scripture references marked KJV are from the Holy Bible: Authorized King James Version.

ISBN: 0-923463-84-4
Printed in the United States of America

INTRODUCTION

PURPOSE

The primary purpose of this curriculum is to encourage consistent Bible reading and memorization for families. It was developed for use at University Park Church, San Bernardino, California. It has been used by many church and home school families with great success. Thanks go to Cathy Duffy, Diana Dogero, Paula Jones, and Dale and Jeannette Walker for their help and encouragement in developing the study and also to Barbara Decker for the inspiration which her book, Proverbs for Parenting, provided.

APPROPRIATE FOR ALL AGES

Designed to reach a variety of age levels, from kindergarten through adult, the study is taken directly from God's Word and, therefore, has the power to convict and instruct both children and adults alike. Besides being a study for families, it also works well as an individual study for adults or older children, as a church or Sunday School curriculum, or as a Family Night program.

Each chapter is a week-long study which is divided into two parts, the introductory lesson and the daily readings. The introductory lesson presents the topic for the week and can stand alone as a complete lesson but will have greater depth if followed up by the daily readings and the summary. There are five verses to memorize each week; the introductory lesson presents the Key Verse, and there are four more verses in the daily readings.

THE AUTHOR

Marty Elwell is a pastor's wife and the mother of four (soon to be five) children. Besides homeschooling for six years, she has teaching experience in the public schools ranging from elementary bilingual education to junior high special education and high school Spanish. She has a Master's Degree in education and has done graduate work at the International School of Theology.

TABLE OF CONTENTS

Section I

USING THE STUDY

USING THE STUDY

READING AND QUESTIONS

The readings are meant to be used on a daily basis and can be read from whatever version of the Bible a family prefers. For consistency the verses in this study are all from the New International Version, and the questions are geared to the wording in that translation. The questions may need to be reworded if you are using a different version of the Bible.

The questions after the word, "DISCUSS," were designed to promote thinking among the family members. These questions may need to be explained, instead of asked, if you are dealing with very young children. The questions after the word, "ANSWER," are just simple comprehension questions about the passage.

Keep in mind that even if a child understands very little of what is being read, you can make it a nice time of being together. The child will be learning at an early age the importance of studying God's Word.

While the Bible passage is being read, be sure to check for understanding. Explain any difficult ideas or words you don't think your children will understand. After you have read the passage, you can have the children tell the story back to you in their own words, with older children adding more detail. Depending on the creativity and desires of your family, you can even have them act out the story or draw it as a group.

BARE BASICS

The titles introducing each daily reading are referred to throughout the study as the Bare Basics. These are short phrases which summarize the daily reading and the memory verse. The Bare Basics can be used as tools to help with recall of memory verses or for young children can memorize it instead of memorizing the Bible verse.

WORKING ON THE RIGHT LEVEL

Families will find it easy to adapt the study to fit their needs. As each family is unique, so is each child. While one child might find it easy to memorize five verses a week, another might struggle with one. Parents must prayerfully consider what will challenge each of their children without overwhelming him. The goal is for consistent, daily family time in the Word of God.

There are basically four levels on which the study can be used. Different members of the family can work on different levels at the same time.

• **Level One** is for very young children. A child at this level would be encouraged to sit and listen quietly while the Bible is being read. Then the story would be retold by an older child or read from a good Bible story book. A very young child would only be expected to repeat back several times the Bare Basic for that reading and/or work every day on memorizing the Key Verse.

• **Level Two** is more challenging, as the child would be expected to memorize the Key Verse and the daily Bare Basic.

• **Level Three** would require memorizing the Key Verse and a shortened portion of each verse (between the [ ] marks) every day.

• **Level Four** requires memorizing the Key Verse and all the daily verses in their entirety.

MEMORIZING SCRIPTURE

It is easier to remember the verses when they are keyed in to both the Bible reference and the Bare Basic. Of course some families may only want to work on one verse a week, the Key Verses from the introductory lessons are ideal for that. Be sure to review the verses on a regular basis. The board game in Appendix D will help your family have fun while reviewing verses. Review each week's verses when you do the summary part of the chapter. Use the Bare Basic and verse reference as a memory clue.

There are many ways to help children (and adults) memorize verses. Some ideas are:

• Have everyone repeat the verse aloud several times together and then check to see if each individual can say it.

• Break the verse into smaller sections, memorize the smaller sections, then put the sections all together.

• Have some sort of body movement or gesture to go with key words in the verse or learn it in sign language.

• Put the verse to rhythm or music.

• Write the verse out on a paper, cut the paper up into pieces, then put them together like a puzzle.

• Use the verse for handwriting or typing practice.

• Go around a circle with each person saying the next word, or toss a ball around with the person catching the ball saying the next word.

• Practice saying the verse while doing exercises, walking around, or jogging in place.

• Write the verse on a chalkboard or dry erase board. Erase one word at a time. Say the verse each time a word is erased. Do this until there are no words left.

• Use the Bare Basic as a clue to the verse. Whoever stands up first gets to say it. Keep score to see who gets the most verses.

• Use the verse as part of your dinner or bedtime prayers.

KEY TO SUCCESS

The key to the success of this study is to adapt it in a way that is comfortable for your family. As children get in the habit of memorizing Scripture, or as they grow older, they can be challenged to achieve more. Don't forget how important parent participation is in the learning process. Be sure to challenge yourself, too. You might even want to have a family Bible quiz.

As stated in the introduction, each chapter is designed as a week-long study. You will notice that there are six parts to each chapter: the introductory lesson, readings 1-4, and the summary. The study was designed with six daily activities so there would be one day each week left free for a make-up or rest day. If your family wants an additional activity for the seventh day, you can either review verses from previous chapters (see the game in Appendix D for a fun way to do this) or work on the craft (see Appendix A) if the craft was not included as part of the introductory lesson. If you find the material in each chapter is too much for your family to cover in one week, then stretch out the chapter over a longer period of time.

The questions for parents at the end of each chapter are included to stimulate parents' thinking on ways to apply this lesson in their children's lives.

MAKING USE OF THE ILLUSTRATIONS

The illustrations were drawn by Steve Rose to bring life to the introductory lesson for each chapter. Extra copies may be made of the illustrations so that each child in the family can color one. You may want to frame some of the colored illustrations, hang them on the refrigerator or bulletin board, or keep them in a notebook as a reminder of the lessons learned. Younger children could color them while the lesson is being taught to help them stay focused.

PERMISSION TO DUPLICATE

Permission is given to duplicate the material contained in this study for family use. Churches or groups must contact the publisher for permission to duplicate any part of this study material.

PLANNING A FAMILY NIGHT OR CLUB

At the back of the study in Appendix A is a list of craft and game ideas to supplement the study. This list was put together to encourage individual families to have a fun family night together or so the study could be used as part of a study time with other families. More information on forming a group family night is included in Appendix B.

MEMORY VERSE CARDS

There are memory verse cards included in Appendix C to cut apart and aid in review of the verses learned.

THE GAME

A SEARCHING FOR TREASURE board game has been developed to give families a fun way to review and retain the verses memorized during the study. The game is found in the back in Appendix D. Instructions for playing and putting the game together are included.

ADDITIONAL STUDIES

Other studies following the same format as **_Searching for Treasure_** are, or will be, available soon. Contact the publisher for information on these studies.

Section II

UNDERSTANDING WISDOM

DEFINING WISDOM

But everyone who hears these words of mine and does not put them into practice is like a foolish man who built his house on sand. The rain came, the streams rose, and the winds blew and beat against that house, and it fell with a great crash.

- Matthew 7:26,27

DEFINING WISDOM

INTRODUCTORY LESSON

DISCUSS: How would you define wisdom? What is the difference between wisdom and knowledge? Can you have a lot of knowledge and still not be wise? How? How do you think God's view of wisdom is different from the way the world sees wisdom? Give some examples if you can.

EXPLAIN: The Bible has a lot to say about wisdom and the wise man. The introductory reading to this week's study is Jesus' description of a wise man. He compares a wise man to a house built on a solid foundation. Discuss how a house is built and focus on the importance of the foundation.

READ: Matthew 7:24-27 (Check for understanding. Clarify any difficult words or concepts.)

DISCUSS: Why did the house built on rock stand firm through the flood? Why did the house on the sand fall down? Why is the person who hears Jesus' words and follows them like the man who built his house on the rock? How do we lay a firm foundation in our lives? What are you doing to lay a good foundation in your life?

PRAY: Pray for your family and the foundation of wisdom on which you want to build your home. Ask God for help in seeing the cracks and weak spots in your family's foundation. Pray that God would show your family His great wisdom as you begin this study and that you would all grow in wisdom and in godly character.

KEY VERSE:

> *The fear of the Lord is*
> *the beginning of wisdom,*
> *and knowledge of the Holy One*
> *is understanding.*
> — *Proverbs 9:10*

READING 1   THE FEAR OF GOD IS THE BEGINNING OF WISDOM

READ: Proverbs 1:1-9

ANSWER: How does wisdom help us? (2-4) What is called the beginning of wisdom? (7) What is it that fools despise? (7) What persons should you listen to? (8)

VERSE: *[The fear of the Lord is the beginning of knowledge,]*
            but fools despise wisdom and discipline. Proverbs 1:7

READING 2   WISDOM IS PROTECTION

READ: Proverbs 2:12-22

ANSWER: What will save you from the ways of wicked men? (12) Describe the different paths of the wise man and the wicked man. (12-15) What is the path you should walk in? (20)

VERSE: *[Wisdom will save you from the ways of wicked men,] from*
            men whose words are perverse. Proverbs 2:12

READING 3   WISDOM IS VERY VALUABLE

READ: Proverbs 3:13-26

ANSWER: What is wisdom more precious than? (14,15) Give a description of wisdom. (17,18) In what does the wise man trust? (26) What isn't the wise man afraid of? (25,26)

VERSE: *[Blessed is the man who finds wisdom,] the man who gains*
            understanding, for she is more profitable than silver and yields
            better returns than gold. Proverbs 3:13,14

READING 4   WISDOM IS FROM GOD

READ: Proverbs 8:1-36

ANSWER: If you fear the Lord, what will you hate? (13) What goes along with
          wisdom? (18) How long has wisdom existed? (23)

VERSE: *[The Lord brought me forth as the first of his works,]*
            before his deeds of old. Proverbs 8:22

SUMMARY

DISCUSS: If someone asked you what wisdom is what would you say?
           Describe why Jesus is the perfect example of wisdom.

APPLY: Make a list of the things that influence you (books, T.V., friends,
           etc.). Determine what paths they will lead you down.

BARE BASICS AND VERSE REVIEW:
          1. The fear of God is the beginning of wisdom (Prov. 1:7)
          2. Wisdom is protection (Prov. 2:12)
          3. Wisdom is very valuable (Prov. 3:13,14)
          4. Wisdom is from God (Prov. 8:22)

QUESTIONS FOR PARENTS

Give examples of important decisions your
children have made. What kind of thinking did
those decisions reflect, the world's or God's?
What do you need to do to train your children to
make wise decisions? How can you use your
own decision making as a teaching tool for your
children?

BECOMING WISE

*At Gibeon the Lord appeared to Solomon
during the night in a dream, and God said,
"Ask for whatever you want me to give you."*
- I Kings 3:5

BECOMING WISE

INTRODUCTORY LESSON

REVIEW: What does the Bible say about wisdom? (Review The Bare Basics and Key Verse.)

DISCUSS: How do you think you get real wisdom? Why would a person want to be wise?

EXPLAIN: King David, the writer of most of the book of Psalms in the Bible, was the most famous king of Israel. He had a son named Solomon who became king after him and was known for his great wisdom and the building of the temple. Solomon wrote three of the books of the Bible: Proverbs, Ecclesiastes, and Song of Songs. Solomon became wise because he asked God for wisdom.

READ: 1 Kings 2:1-4; 3:4-15 (Check for understanding. Clarify any difficult words or concepts.)

DISCUSS: What did God promise to do for David if his descendants were faithful to Him in the way they lived? What do you think God planned to do if they weren't faithful? Why did Solomon ask God for wisdom? Why did God give Solomon what he asked for? Have you ever asked God for wisdom? Has he answered your prayer? How? What do you need to do to get wisdom?

PRAY: Pray that you and your family will want wisdom and that God will give it to you. Pray for wisdom in any major decisions you need to make and for daily wisdom in all the little choices you face each day. Thank God for revealing Himself to you and your family and acknowledge that knowing Him is the beginning of wisdom.

KEY VERSE:

> *Listen, my sons,*
> *to a father's instruction;*
> *pay attention and gain understanding.*
> *— Proverbs 4:1*

READING 1   GOD GIVES WISDOM

READ: Proverbs 2:l-ll

ANSWER: Who gives wisdom? (6) The search for wisdom is compared to what? (4) Can you get wisdom without seeking after it? How should you seek wisdom?

VERSE: *[For the Lord gives wisdom, and from his mouth come knowledge and understanding.]* Proverbs 2:6

READING 2   TRUST GOD FOR WISDOM

READ: Proverbs 3:1-12

ANSWER: How will keeping God's commands affect your life? (2) If you trust God, what will He do? (5,6) Who does God discipline? (l2)

VERSE: *[Trust in the Lord with all your heart and lean not on your own understanding;] in all your ways acknowledge him, and he will make your paths straight.* Proverbs 3:5,6

READING 3   SEEK TO GAIN WISDOM

READ: Proverbs 4:l-9

ANSWER: Is there anything more valuable than wisdom? (7) To get wisdom what should you do? (l,l0) What will wisdom do for you if you embrace her? (8,9)

VERSE: *[Wisdom is supreme; therefore get wisdom.] Though it cost all you have, get understanding.* Proverbs 4:7

READING 4   BE TEACHABLE

READ: Proverbs 9:1-12

ANSWER: If you teach a wise man, what will happen to him? (8,9) What happens if you try to teach a wicked man? (7,8) What is understanding? (10)

VERSE: *[Instruct a wise man and he will be wiser still;] teach a righteous man and he will add to his learning.* Proverbs 9:9

SUMMARY

DISCUSS: Think of a person from the Bible who was wise. Describe the way he obtained wisdom. Are you seeking wisdom with all your heart? What gets in the way of your seeking wisdom?

APPLY: Write down what steps you can take to become wiser. Pray that you will desire wisdom more than the things of the world.

BARE BASICS AND VERSE REVIEW:
    1. God gives wisdom (Prov 2:6)
    2. Trust God for wisdom (Prov. 3:5,6)
    3. Seek to gain wisdom (Prov. 4:7)
    4. Be teachable (Prov. 9:9)

QUESTIONS FOR PARENTS

What evidence can you give that seeking after wisdom is important to your children? How do you encourage them to seek wisdom? What steps can you take to encourage them, even more, to seek wisdom?

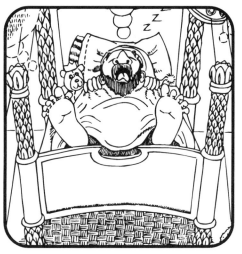

RECOGNIZING THE WISE MAN

But Daniel resolved not to defile himself
with the royal food and wine,
and he asked the chief official for permission
not to defile himself this way.
- Daniel 1:8

RECOGNIZING THE WISE MAN

INTRODUCTORY LESSON

REVIEW: What does the Bible say about becoming wise? (Review The Bare Basics and Key Verse.)

DISCUSS: What makes a man wise? What would be a good description of a wise man? Can you give any examples of men or women from the Bible or from history who were wise? What did they do to show they were wise?

EXPLAIN: During one period of time when the people of Israel were very disobedient to God, he made them leave the land He had given them and go as captives into the land of Babylon. The kings of Judah and the people had been disobedient and worshiped other gods. God had warned them through his prophets that he would have to punish them. There were some people who remained faithful to God and whom God blessed. One faithful man was Daniel who became an adviser to the kings of Babylon. He was only a teenager when he was taken captive.

READ: Daniel, Chapter 1 (Check for understanding. Clarify any difficult words or concepts.)

DISCUSS: Why was Daniel chosen to be trained for the king's service? What do you think was wrong with the king's food? Do you think it was easy for Daniel to say he wouldn't eat the king's food? Why do you think he was able to take such a stand? Why did the chief official respond favorably to Daniel's request to be given other food? What was the result of Daniel's obedience to God?

PRAY: Pray that everyone in your family will grow in wisdom and reflect God in their lives. Pray for greater understanding of God's Word, a willingness to listen to God, and an openness to discipline and correction.

KEY VERSE:

> *A wise man fears the Lord and shuns evil,*
> *but a fool is hotheaded and reckless.*
> *- Proverbs 14:16*

READING 1   A WISE MAN STANDS FIRM

READ: Proverbs 10:14-25

ANSWER: What do wise men store up? (14) Describe the tongue of the wise man. (19-21) What happens to the righteous man in a storm? (25)

VERSE: *When the storm has swept by, the wicked are gone, but [the righteous stand firm forever.]* Proverbs 10:25

READING 2   A WISE MAN LOVES DISCIPLINE

READ: Proverbs 12:1-8

ANSWER: What does the wise man love? (1) What does a good man receive from God? (2) Describe a noble wife. (4)

VERSE: *[Whoever loves discipline loves knowledge,] but he who hates correction is stupid.* Proverbs 12:1

READING 3   A WISE MAN FEARS GOD

READ: Proverbs 14:1-3, 8-9, 15-16, 26-27

ANSWER: How do you think a wise woman builds her house? (1) What does it mean to "give thought to your ways"? (8,15) What would a secure fortress be like? (26)

VERSE: *[The fear of the Lord is a fountain of life,] turning a man from the snares of death.* Proverbs 14:27

READING 4   A WISE MAN LISTENS

READ: Proverbs 16:6-7, 12-13, 16-17, 20-24

ANSWER: What kind of man does a king value? Why? (13) Why is getting wisdom better than gold or silver? (16)   What does it mean to be discerning? (21)

VERSE: *[Whoever gives heed to instruction prospers,] and blessed is he who trusts in the Lord.* Proverbs 16:20

SUMMARY

DISCUSS: Find an example in the Bible of someone who God disciplined and became wiser because of God's discipline. What is a description of a wise man?

APPLY: Does your life show you are a wise person? Pray that God will help you become wiser. When you are disciplined be grateful and ask God to help you become wiser through it.

BARE BASICS AND VERSE REVIEW:
        1. A wise man stands firm (Prov. 10:25)
        2. A wise man loves discipline (Prov. 12:1)
        3. A wise man fears God (Prov. 14:27)
        4. A wise man listens (Prov. 16:20)

QUESTIONS FOR PARENTS

What adjectives would you use to describe your children? Are these characteristics of a wise person? What can you do to encourage the growth of wisdom in your children?

THE FOOLISH MAN

*But Rehoboam rejected the advice
the elders gave him and consulted the young men
who had grown up with him and were serving him.*
- *2 Chronicles 10:8*

STAYING AWAY FROM THE FOOLISH MAN

INTRODUCTORY LESSON

REVIEW: How does the Bible describe a person with wisdom? (Review The Bare Basics and Key Verse.)

DISCUSS: How would you describe a person without wisdom? How do you tell the difference between a wise person and a fool? Can you think of examples of foolish or wicked people? What happened to these people? What happened to their families?

EXPLAIN: King Solomon was known for his great wisdom. When he died his son Rehoboam became king. Rehoboam was not wise. He rejected the advice of the older men who had served his father and instead listened to young men who had no experience. As a result of his foolishness Rehoboam lost most of his kingdom.

READ: 2 Chronicles 9:30 - 10:19 (Check for understanding. Clarify any difficult words or concepts.)

DISCUSS: What was the problem the people of Israel had with Solomon? What did they want Rehoboam to do? What advice did Rehoboam get? Who do you think gave the best advice? Why? Why do you think Rehoboam chose to treat the people the way he did? What happened because of Rehoboam's choice? What do you think would have happened if he had lightened the load of the people instead of responding the way he did? How would you describe Rehoboam?

PRAY: Pray that God would give each one of you wisdom to see when you are making foolish decisions. Pray for wisdom in choosing friends and advisers. Thank God that his Word shows us what happens when we make good choices and what happens when we make bad choices. Thank God that when you follow him you will be wise.

KEY VERSE:

> *A fool finds pleasure in evil conduct,*
> *but a man of understanding*
> *delights in wisdom.*
> *- Proverbs 10:23*

READING 1   A FOOL WILL BE DESTROYED

READ: Proverbs 1:20-33

ANSWER: What will wisdom do to the person who ignores her? (25,26) What will be the end of the fool? (32) What does it mean to eat the "fruit of their ways"? (31)

VERSE: *For [the waywardness of the simple will kill them,] and the complacency of fools will destroy them.* Proverbs 1:32

READING 2   A WICKED MAN WILL GET CAUGHT

READ: Proverbs 5:1-23

ANSWER: What path does an adulteress lead people down? (5,6) When you don't obey your teachers what happens? (13,14) What does God see? (21)

VERSE: *[The evil deeds of a wicked man ensnare him;] the cords of his sin hold him fast.* Proverbs 5:22

READING 3   A FOOL WILL BE PUNISHED

READ: Proverbs 10:7-13, 27-32

ANSWER: What does it mean that the name of the wicked will rot? (7) What is a rod used for? (13) Describe the end of the wicked. (28-30)

VERSE: *Wisdom is found on the lips of the discerning, but [a rod is for the back of him who lacks judgment.]* Proverbs 10:13

READING 4   A FOOL HATES INSTRUCTION AND HIMSELF

READ: Proverbs 15:3, 5, 8-12, 32-33

ANSWER: Describe the difference between the way God looks at the wicked and the righteous. (8,9) What happens to the man who leaves God's path? (10) How does the man who ignores discipline think of himself? (32)

VERSE: *[He who ignores discipline despises himself,] but whoever heeds correction gains understanding.* Proverbs 15:32

SUMMARY

DISCUSS: What is the path like that the man without wisdom follows? Why would a person reject wisdom? Who is a person in the Bible who left God's path? What happened to that person?

APPLY: Describe one way your parents' discipline has helped you avoid the path of a man without wisdom.

BARE BASICS AND VERSE REVIEW:
    1. A fool will be destroyed (Prov. 1:32)
    2. A wicked man will get caught (Prov. 5:22)
    3. A fool will be punished (Prov. 10:13)
    4. A fool hates instruction and himself (Prov. 15:32)

QUESTIONS FOR PARENTS

What are some of the foolish things your children have done? How can you get them to recognize when their behavior is foolish? How can you use some of the foolish things you have done to teach your children?

Section III

DEVELOPING RIGHT RELATIONSHIPS

CHOOSING YOUR FRIENDS

When Delilah saw that he had told her everything, she sent word to the rulers of the Philistines, "Come back once more; he has told me everything." So the rulers of the Philistines returned with the silver in their hands. Having put him to sleep on her lap, she called a man to shave off the seven braids of his hair, and so began to subdue him.
And his strength left him.
- Judges 16:18,19

CHOOSING YOUR FRIENDS

INTRODUCTORY LESSON

REVIEW: What does the Bible say about the foolish man? (Review The Bare Basics and Key Verse.)

PRESENT: Have some of the family do a presentation on different ways of choosing friends.

DISCUSS: What is it we need to look at when we choose who will be our friends? Why is who we choose as a friend important? Why do we choose people to be our friends who will be a bad influence on us?

EXPLAIN: Samson was one of the judges of Israel before there were kings. He had been set aside for God from birth. He was a Nazirite, which means separated or dedicated. As a Nazirite he could not drink wine or other alcohol or shave his hair. Samson was a man of extraordinary strength, empowered by God. He also had a weakness for women and did not choose wisely who he would be with. God had warned his people not to take for themselves foreign wives. The woman in the story is not Samson's wife, which in itself is a sin. She is also a Philistine. The Philistines were the enemies of God.

READ: Judges 16:1-22 (Check for understanding. Clarify any difficult words or concepts.)

DISCUSS: How can you tell that Delilah was not a good friend to Samson? Why couldn't Samson see that she was trying to destroy him? What was the symbol of Samson's strength? What was the real source of his strength? If Samson had chosen his friends wisely, how would the story of his life have been different? What kind of wife should Samson have chosen?

PRAY: Thank God that He has given you His word to guide and instruct. Pray for wisdom and insight in choosing friends. Ask for help in choosing friends who will encourage you in your walk with God.

KEY VERSE:

> *What harmony is there between Christ and Belial? What does a believer have in common with an unbeliever?*
> *- 2 Corinthians 6:15*
> *(Belial is a Hebrew word for Satan.)*

READING 1   YOU BECOME LIKE YOUR FRIENDS

READ: Proverbs 4:14,15; 13:20; 22:24,25

ANSWER: Who grows wise? Who suffers harm? (13:20) Why shouldn't you associate with a hot-tempered person? (22:24,25)

VERSE: *[He who walks with the wise grows wise, but a companion of fools suffers harm.]* Proverbs 13:20

READING 2   BAD FRIENDS HURT YOUR CHARACTER

READ: Romans 16:17-19; 1 Corinthians 15:33-34

ANSWER: What does naive mean? How are naive people deceived? How can you keep yourself from being deceived? Why do you think that bad company corrupts good character?   (1 Cor. 15:33)

VERSE: *Do not be misled: ["Bad company corrupts good character."]*
          1 Corinthians 15:33

READING 3   DON'T BE YOKED WITH UNBELIEVERS

READ: 2 Corinthians 6:14-18

ANSWER: What do you think it means to be yoked together with an unbeliever? Why don't believers and unbelievers have anything in common? If we belong to God, how should we be different from other people?

VERSE: *[Do not be yoked together with unbelievers.] For what do righteousness and wickedness have in common? Or what fellowship can light have with darkness?* 2 Corinthians 6:14

READING 4   DON'T ASSOCIATE WITH EVIL PEOPLE

READ: Ephesians 5:1-17

ANSWER: Why doesn't an immoral, impure or greedy person have any inheritance in the kingdom of God? (5) How do we understand what the will of God is? (17) How do you live as a wise person? (15)

VERSE: *[Have nothing to do with the fruitless deeds of darkness,] but rather expose them.* Ephesians 5:11

SUMMARY

DISCUSS: What are some characteristics people might have that you should avoid? Have you seen someone who has gotten in trouble because of the company he/she kept?

APPLY: Are you friends with a person who has the characteristics you think you should avoid? If you are, what should you do about it?

BARE BASICS AND VERSE REVIEW:
1. You become like your friends (Prov. 13:20)
2. Bad friends hurt your character (1 Cor. 15:33)
3. Don't be yoked with unbelievers (2 Cor. 6:14)
4. Don't associate with evil people (Eph. 5:11)

QUESTIONS FOR PARENTS

Describe your children's choice of friends. What does their choice of friends show about their judgment? What can you do to help your children learn to be wise in their choice of friends?

BEING A FRIEND

In the morning Jonathan went out to the field for his meeting with David. He had a small boy with him, and he said to the boy, "Run and find the arrows I shoot."
- 1 Samuel 20:35,36a

BEING A FRIEND

INTRODUCTORY LESSON

REVIEW: What does the Bible say about choosing a friend? (Review The Bare Basics and Key Verse.)

PRESENT: Have some of the family do a presentation on what a friend should be like.

DISCUSS: Why is having friends important? What makes a person a good friend? How do you know if a friend can be trusted? What happens when friends can't be trusted?

EXPLAIN: King Saul was the first king of Israel. He turned away from God and was very disobedient. The prophet Samuel told him that God was going to take the throne away from his family and give it to David. Saul hated David and kept trying to kill him. Saul's own son, Jonathan, was David's friend. He was a good friend and was not even jealous that David would be king instead of him. He showed true friendship for David as he tried to protect him from Saul.

READ: 1 Samuel, Chapter 20 (Check for understanding. Clarify any difficult words or concepts.)

DISCUSS: Why didn't Jonathan believe David at first when David said that Saul was trying to kill him? What convinced Jonathan that what David said about Saul was true? Why did Saul want to kill David? What was Jonathan's response to Saul? How did Jonathan show he was David's good friend?

PRAY: Thank God for the good friends he has given you. Thank him for people in the past who have really helped you out and demonstrated real friendship. Ask God to help you be a good friend to others, that you would be trustworthy and willing to make sacrifices to help them.

KEY VERSE:

A friend loves at all times,
and a brother is born for adversity.
- Proverbs 17:17

READING 1   A FRIEND CAN BE TRUSTED

READ: Proverbs 18:24; 27:6,9,10

ANSWER: Explain verse 17:17 in your own words. What does it mean that wounds from a friend can be trusted? (27:6) What does it mean to forsake a friend? (27:10)

VERSE: *[Wounds from a friend can be trusted,] but an enemy multiplies kisses.* Proverbs 27:6

READING 2   A FRIEND IS HELPFUL

READ: Ecclesiastes 4:9-12

ANSWER: Why are two people better than one? (9,10) Why can't a cord of three strands be broken easily? (12) How does the three strand cord relate to friendship?

VERSE: *[If one falls down, his friend can help him up.] But pity the man who falls and has no one to help him up.* Ecclesiastes 4:10

READING 3   A FRIEND MAKES SACRIFICES

READ: John 15:12-17

ANSWER: What is the greatest way a person can show love for another? (13) Did Jesus show love that way? How? What is Jesus' command to us? (17) In what way are we to love one another? (12)

VERSE: *[Greater love has no man than this, that he lay down his life for his friends.]* John 15:13

READING 4   A FRIEND SHOWS LOVE

READ: Romans 13:8-10

ANSWER: What is the only debt we are to have? (8) What is the one commandment that sums up all the others? (19) Love doesn't do what? (10)

VERSE: *[Love does no harm to its neighbor.] Therefore love is the fulfillment of the law.* Romans 13:10

SUMMARY

DISCUSS: What are the characteristics you should look for in a friend? Do you have friends who will stand by you no matter what? Think of a time when a friend has really helped you out.

APPLY: Look at what kind of a friend you are. How do you think you could be a better friend?

BARE BASICS AND VERSE REVIEW:
        1. A friend can be trusted (Prov. 27:6)
        2. A friend is helpful (Ecc. 4:10)
        3. A friend makes sacrifices (John 15:13)
        4. A friend shows love (Rom. 13:10)

QUESTIONS FOR PARENTS

How have your children demonstrated that they are good friends? What are some of the problems that your children have had in friendships? What can you do to train them to be better friends?

HONORING YOUR PARENTS

So he said to them, "Why do you do such things?
I hear from all the people about these wicked deeds of yours.
No, my sons; it is not a good report that I hear spreading among the
Lord's people. If a man sins against another man,
God may mediate for him; but if a man sins against the Lord, who will
intercede for him?" His sons, however, did not listen to their father's
rebuke, for it was the Lord's will to put them to death.
- 1 Samuel 2:23-25

HONORING YOUR PARENTS

INTRODUCTORY LESSON

REVIEW: What does the Bible say about being a friend? (Review The Bare Basics and Key Verse.)

PRESENT: Have some of the family do a presentation on good and bad ways to respond to your parents.

DISCUSS: Why is obeying your parents important? What causes problems between parents and children? What are the parents' responsibilities toward their children? What are the children's responsibilities toward their parents?

EXPLAIN: During the time Eli was priest in Israel, a woman named Hannah came to the temple to pray for a son, as she had no children. The Lord answered her prayer and gave her a son, Samuel, who she brought back to the temple to serve the Lord with Eli. Samuel grew to be a godly man, but Eli's own sons were disobedient to their father and rebellious against God. The sad thing is that Samuel saw what happened to Eli's sons and then didn't raise his own sons any differently.

READ: 1 Samuel 2:12-36 (Check for understanding. Clarify any difficult words or concepts.)

DISCUSS: What showed the wickedness of Eli's sons? Why wouldn't Eli's sons listen to their father? What should Eli have done about his sons? What did God say would happen to Eli's sons? (Read 1 Samuel 4:12-18 to see what happened.)

PRAY: Pray for wisdom to lead your children into a right relationship with God and discernment to discipline them correctly. Pray that your children's hearts would be turned to the Lord, that they would learn from discipline, and that they would want to be obedient to their parents. Thank God for the family he has given you and that His Word shows you how you can learn to get along.

KEY VERSE:

> *The eye that mocks a father,*
> *that scorns obedience to a mother,*
> *will be pecked out by the ravens of the valley,*
> *will be eaten by the vultures.*
> *- Proverbs 30:17*

READING 1   LISTEN TO YOUR PARENTS

READ: Proverbs 4:10-12; 6:20-23; 15:5,20; 23:24,25

ANSWER: To whom should you listen? Why? Who has great joy? (23:24)
Why? A person who doesn't listen to a father's advice is what? (15:5)
What are you?

VERSE: *My son, [keep your father's commands] and do not forsake your mother's teaching.* Proverbs 6:20

READING 2   HONOR YOUR PARENTS

READ: Exodus 20:12

ANSWER: If you honor your father and mother, what will be the result?

VERSE: *[Honor your father and your mother,] so that you may live long in the land the Lord your God is giving you.* Exodus 20:12

READING 3   OBEY YOUR PARENTS IN THE LORD

READ: Ephesians 6:1-4

ANSWER: What are children to do? (1) What are fathers supposed to do? (4)
If a father doesn't do what God says, is a child still supposed to
obey? What will be the result if the child obeys?

VERSE: *[Children, obey your parents in the Lord,] for this is right.*
Ephesians 6:1

READING 4   OBEY YOUR PARENTS IN EVERYTHING

READ: Colossians 3:18-25

ANSWER: What is the command for wives? (18) What is the command for husbands? (19) What is the command for children? (20) Why are we to obey these commands? (20,23)

VERSE: *[Children, obey your parents in everything,] for this pleases the Lord.*
Colossians 3:20

SUMMARY

DISCUSS: Why do you think God wants you to listen to your parents? If you think your parents are wrong about something, what should you do?

APPLY: Be aware of any time this week when you did not listen to your parents. Tell your parents you're sorry and also confess this to God.

BARE BASICS AND VERSE REVIEW:
        1. Listen to your parents (Prov. 23:24)
        2. Honor your parents (Ex. 20:12)
        3. Obey your parents in the Lord (Eph. 6:1)
        4. Obey your parents in everything (Col. 3:20)

QUESTIONS FOR PARENTS

What are some things your children have done recently which show honor to you? What are some examples of how they dishonor you? What steps do you need to take to bring them into greater obedience to both you and God? How can you help them develop an attitude of honor?

Section IV

CONTROLLING YOURSELF

CONTROLLING YOUR ANGER

Now Cain said to his brother Abel, "Let's go out to the field." And while they were in the field, Cain attacked his brother Abel and killed him.

Genesis 4:8

CONTROLLING YOUR ANGER

INTRODUCTORY LESSON

REVIEW: What does the Bible say about honoring your parents? (Review The Bare Basics and Key Verse.)

PRESENT: Have one of the family put on an act of an angry person.

DISCUSS: What happens when a person gets angry? What effect does an angry person have on the people around him? Why do people get angry? Does anger help people get what they want? Does it ever make a situation better?

EXPLAIN: Adam and Eve were the first man and woman and were created by God. Their first two sons were Cain and Abel. When they brought offerings to God, God was pleased with Abel's offering but not Cain's. Remember that God looks at a person's heart and his motivation. Abel brought the offering God wanted him to bring. Cain brought the offering he wanted rather than what God wanted. Then Cain got angry because God was not pleased with his offering.

READ: Genesis 4:1-12 (Check for understanding. Clarify any difficult words or concepts.)

DISCUSS: What was the difference between the offerings of Cain and Abel? Why was Abel's offering pleasing to God and not Cain's? (Focus on Cain bringing some of his fruit while Abel brought from the first-born. God wants us to set aside the best for Him first.) Why did Cain get angry? Did Cain have a good reason to get angry? What did God say to Cain when he got angry? Did Cain listen to God? Because Cain didn't want to control his anger, what terrible sin did he commit? What was the punishment for what he did?

PRAY: Pray that God would show you how destructive anger is. Ask for help in controlling anger and responding correctly when someone or something makes you mad. Have everyone ask for forgiveness for a specific time they got angry and either hurt someone else or did something wrong.

KEY VERSE:

> *A gentle answer turns away wrath,*
> *but a harsh word stirs up anger.*
> *- Proverbs 15:1*

READING 1　　　A WISE MAN AVOIDS ANGER

READS:　　　Proverbs 12:16; 14:16-17; 15:18

ANSWER:　　What is the difference between a fool and a righteous man? Responding in anger causes a person to do what kind of things? (14:17) What is it that stirs up anger? (15:1) What is it that calms anger? (15:1)

VERSE:　　*A fool shows his annoyance at once, but [a prudent man overlooks an insult.]* Proverbs 12:16

READING 2　　　AN ANGRY MAN WILL SIN

READS:　　　Proverbs 22:24,25; 25:28; 29:22

ANSWER:　　With whom shouldn't you associate and why? (22:24,25) What would happen to a city whose walls are broken down? (25:28) What is one way you can avoid committing sin? (29:22)

VERSE:　　*[An angry man stirs up dissension,] and a hot-tempered one commits many sins.* Proverbs 29:22

READING 3　　　GOD JUDGES OUR ANGER

READS:　　　Matthew 5:21-24

ANSWER:　　Why is it so bad to be angry and say bad things about other people? (22) What should you do if you have a problem with another person? (23,24)

VERSE:　　*But I tell you that [anyone who is angry with his brother will be subject to judgment.]* Matthew 5:22a

READING 4   ANGER DOES NOT HONOR GOD

READ: James 1:19-25

ANSWER: What are the things we should be slow to do? (19) What do you think it means that "man's anger does not bring about the righteous life God desires"? (20) What does it mean to do what the Word says? (22,23)

VERSE: *Everyone should be quick to listen, slow to speak, and slow to become angry, for [man's anger does not bring about the righteous life that God desires.]* James 1:19,20

SUMMARY

DISCUSS: What makes you the most angry, and what steps can you take to control your anger?

APPLY: When you find yourself getting angry, take a deep breath and repeat to yourself one of the verses you have memorized.

BARE BASICS AND VERSE REVIEW:
        1. A wise man avoids anger (Prov. 12:16)
        2. An angry man will sin (Prov. 29:22)
        3. God judges our anger (Matt. 5:22a)
        4. Anger does not honor God
              (James 1:19,20)

QUESTIONS FOR PARENTS

What are your children trying to accomplish when they get mad? What happens to children when they get their way? What are the best ways to react to your children's anger? What are some ways to teach your children that anger doesn't work?

GIVING UP YOUR PRIDE

*Suddenly the fingers of a human hand appeared
and wrote on the plaster of the wall,
near the lampstand in the royal palace.
The king watched the hand as it wrote.
His face turned pale and he was so frightened that his
knees knocked together and his legs gave way.*
- Daniel 5:5,6

GIVING UP YOUR PRIDE

INTRODUCTORY LESSON

REVIEW: What does the Bible say about anger? (Review The Bare Basics and Key Verse.)

PRESENT: Have one of the family put on an act of a prideful person.

DISCUSS: What does it mean to be proud? How do prideful people affect other people? How does God view people who are proud?

EXPLAIN: When the Jewish people were exiled to Babylon, they were first under the rule of Nebuchadnezzar. God used Nebuchadnezzar to punish His people for the sins they committed. Nebuchadnezzar was proud and took credit for what God had given him, and so God punished him. In this reading Belshazzar is now on the throne. He didn't learn anything from what happened to Nebuchadnezzar, and God had to deal with his pride too.

READ: Daniel, Chapter 5 (Check for understanding. Clarify any difficult words or concepts.)

DISCUSS: What was Belshazzar doing that made God angry? What did the things Belshazzar was doing show about him? What had happened to Nebuchadnezzar? Why had this happened? Why didn't Belshazzar learn anything from what happened to Nebuchadnezzar? Does God always punish the proud right away like that? What are some ways the proud are punished?

PRAY: Thank God for showing you so clearly in His Word how He hates pride. Ask Him to show you areas of pride in your life. Confess any pride you can see. Ask God for a right view of who you are and who He is.

KEY VERSE:

> *The eyes of the arrogant man will be humbled and the pride of men brought low; the Lord alone will be exalted in that day.*
>
> *Isaiah 2:11*

READING 1   A PRIDEFUL PERSON WILL FALL

READ: Proverbs 16:5,18,19; 18:11,12

ANSWER: Who does God detest, and what will happen to them? (16:5)
Explain verse 16:18 in your own words. Who is it God will honor?
(18:12)

VERSE: *[Pride goes before destruction,] and a haughty spirit before a fall.*
Proverbs 16:18

READING 2   GOOD THINGS COME FROM GOD

READ: Deuteronomy 8:10-20

ANSWER: If we forget to praise God for good things, what will happen to
us? (10-14) Who is the source of all things? (18) What will happen
to us if we become prideful and forget who is the source of all
things? (19,20)

VERSE: *When you have eaten and are satisfied, [praise the Lord your God
for the good land he has given you.]* Deuteronomy 8:10

READING 3   DON'T TRUST IN YOURSELF

READ: Isaiah 2:6-22

ANSWER: In the end, who will be exalted and who will be brought low? (11)
Describe what will happen when God reveals the splendor of His
majesty? (10,19) In whom should we trust? (22) Why?

VERSE: *[Stop trusting in man,] who has but a breath in his nostrils. Of what
account is he?* Isaiah 2:22

READING 4   THE PROUD WILL BE HUMBLED

READ: Matthew 23:1-12

ANSWER: Are we to do things for other men to see (to get them to think we are great)? (5) Who do you think we should try to please? Who does God consider the greatest among us? (11) To be exalted, what do we first need to do? (12) What do you think that means?

VERSE: *For [whoever exalts himself will be humbled,] and whoever humbles himself will be exalted.* Matthew 23:12

SUMMARY

DISCUSS: List ways that people are proud and how they tend to forget about God. What would happen to mankind if God moved the earth just a little closer to the sun? Does man really have anything to be proud of?

APPLY: Look for an area in your life where you tend to be proud. (Hint: When you criticize others, you are probably proud in the area that you are criticizing.) Confess this to God and ask Him to give you a humble heart.

BARE BASICS AND VERSE REVIEW:
   1. A prideful person will fall (Prov. 16:18)
   2. Good things come from God (Deut.8:10)
   3. Don't trust in yourself (Isa. 2:22)
   4. The proud will be humbled
                              (Matt. 23:12)

QUESTIONS FOR PARENTS

What are some of the ways your children show evidence of pride in their lives? How can you help them look at themselves in a realistic and appropriate manner? How can you encourage them in the areas where God has gifted them without promoting pride?

OVERCOMING TEMPTATION

Again, the devil took him to a very high mountain and showed him all the kingdoms of the world and their splendor. "All this I will give you," he said, "if you will bow down and worship me." Jesus said to him, "Away from me, Satan! For it is written: 'Worship the Lord your God, and serve him only.'"
- Matthew 4:8-10

OVERCOMING TEMPTATION

INTRODUCTORY LESSON

REVIEW: What does the Bible say about pride? (Review The Bare Basics and Key Verse.)

PRESENT: Have one of the family act out someone giving into a temptation.

DISCUSS: What is temptation? Is temptation a sin? What is the problem we have with temptation? What area is Satan most likely to tempt you in? How can you overcome temptation?

EXPLAIN: At the beginning of Jesus' public ministry, He spent 40 days in the wilderness fasting and praying. He hadn't eaten for 40 days and was in a very weak condition. Satan knew that if he could get Jesus to sin then Jesus would not be pure and able to die for the sins of others. Because Jesus was filled with the Holy Spirit He did not give into temptation; instead He came against the temptations of Satan with the truth of God's Word.

READ: Matthew 4:1-11 (Check for understanding. Clarify any difficult words or concepts.)

DISCUSS: How hungry do you think Jesus was? Could He have turned the stones into bread? How do you know? (Remember the bread and the fishes, Mark 6:30-44.) Does Satan have the power to make someone a ruler in this world? (Think about the anti-Christ, Revelations ch.13.) Did Jesus come as a king? If He had given into Satan, would people have rejected Him like they did? Why or why not? Can Jesus understand our temptations? How do you know? How was Jesus strengthened after His confrontation with Satan and temptation?

PRAY: Ask for help in identifying weak areas of your life where you are vulnerable to temptation. Pray for strength to resist in those areas. Pray for the power to respond to temptation in the way that Jesus did.

KEY VERSE:

> *For we do not have a high priest who is unable to sympathize with our weaknesses, but we have one who was tempted in every way, just as we are - yet without sin.*
> *- Hebrews 4:15*

READING 1   DO NOT GIVE IN TO SIN

READ: Proverbs 1:10-19

ANSWER: If someone tries to get you to do something wrong, what should you do? (10, 15) How do you think we know what is wrong to do? What happens to people who do things in a bad way? (19)

VERSE: *My son, [if sinners entice you, do not give in to them.] Proverbs 1:10*

READING 2   GOD WILL HELP YOU OVERCOME TEMPTATION

READ: 1 Corinthians 10:1-13

ANSWER: Why wasn't God pleased with the Israelites? (6-10) For what are they an example to us? (6-11) When should we be most careful not to fall into temptation? (12)

VERSE: *No temptation has seized you except what is common to man. And [God is faithful; he will not let you be tempted beyond what you can bear.] But when you are tempted, he will also provide a way out so that you can stand up under it. 1 Corinthians 10:13*

READING 3   GOD UNDERSTANDS OUR NEEDS

READ: Hebrews 4:14-16

ANSWER: Who understands our weaknesses? (15) What happened to Jesus when he was tempted to sin? (15) When we are tempted to sin, what can we do? (16) What will be the result? (16)

VERSE: *[Let us then approach the throne of grace with confidence, so that we may receive mercy and find grace to help us in our time of need.] Hebrews 4:16*

READING 4   GOD DOES NOT TEMPT US

READ: James 1:13-15

ANSWER: If God doesn't tempt us to do evil, who or what does? (14) If we
               give into temptation, what is the result? (15) What is the end result
               of sin? (15) Do you think that is what God wants for you?

VERSE: *When tempted, no one should say, "God is tempting me." For [God
               cannot be tempted by evil, nor does he tempt anyone.]* James 1:13

SUMMARY

DISCUSS: Define temptation. Into what are areas of temptation do people
               tend to fall?

APPLY: What is your greatest temptation? Pray for strength to overcome in
               this area. When you are tempted this week recite 1 Corinthians
               10:13 and then pray to see the way out that God provides.

BARE BASICS AND VERSE REVIEW:
               1. Do not give into sin (Prov. 1:10)
               2. God will help you overcome temptation (1 Cor. 10:13)
               3. God understands our needs (Heb. 4:16)
               4. God does not tempt us (James 1:13)

QUESTIONS FOR PARENTS

What are some of the temptations which your
children face? When are your children most
likely to give into temptation? What are some
ways you can help them overcome temptations?

Section V

CONTROLLING WHAT YOU SAY

ARGUING AND COMPLAINING

The Lord said to Moses and Aaron: "How long will this wicked community grumble against me? I have heard the complaints of these grumbling Israelites. So tell them, 'As surely as I live, declares the Lord, I will do to you the very things I heard you say: In this desert your bodies will fall - every one of you twenty years old or more who was counted in the census and who has grumbled against me.'"
- Numbers 14:26-29

ARGUING AND COMPLAINING

INTRODUCTORY LESSON

REVIEW: What does the Bible teach us about temptation? (Review The Bare Basics and Key Verse.)

PRESENT: Have some of the family present what goes on in an argument.

DISCUSS: How does an argument get started? What keeps an argument going? How can an argument be stopped? What is the difference between arguing and complaining? What does complaining show about a person? What does complaining achieve?

EXPLAIN: God brought His people Israel out of Egypt where they had been slaves. He performed great miracles and showed them His power and mercy, but they still did not want to trust Him. They sent out spies to check out the land they were about to enter. The report of the spies made the people afraid. They started to grumble against God, as they didn't want to enter the land He had promised to give them.

READ: Numbers 14:1-35 (Check for understanding. Clarify any difficult words or concepts.)

DISCUSS: Why were the people afraid to enter the land? What did Joshua and Caleb say about the land and its people? What did God want to do to the Israelites? What was Moses' response to God? The complaints of the people were a sin against God, and God forgave them, but what was the consequence of their sin? Why did God hate their grumbling so much? What happened to Joshua and Caleb?

PRAY: Thank God that He is over all things and completely trustworthy. Ask Him to help you be satisfied in all things and learn to do everything without complaining or arguing. Ask Him to make you aware of your wrong attitudes and pray for a heart to want to make things right.

KEY VERSE:

A fool's lips bring him strife,
and his mouth invites a beating.
- Proverbs 18:6

READING 1 — AVOID AN ARGUMENT

READ: Proverbs 17:1,14,19; 20:3; 25:24; 26:17,20,21

ANSWER: Why is it better to have very little and have a peaceful house than to have a lot of things but have a house full of arguing? (17:1) Who is quick to quarrel? (20:3) What happens to a fire when there is no wood? How does that relate to a quarrel? (26:20)

VERSE: *[It is to a man's honor to avoid strife,] but every fool is quick to quarrel.* Proverbs 20:3

READING 2 — DO EVERYTHING WITHOUT COMPLAINING OR ARGUING

READ: Philippians 2:14-16

ANSWER: Why should we do things without complaining? (14,15) What makes us shine like stars? (15,16) How is the world described? (15)

VERSE: *[Do everything without complaining or arguing,] so that you may become blameless and pure, children of God without fault in a crooked and depraved generation.* Philippians 2:14,15

READING 3 — DO WHAT IS GOOD

READ: Titus 3:1-11

ANSWER: What are some things we need to do? (1,2) What are we supposed to avoid? (9) A person who causes trouble between others (divisive) is described in what way? (10,11)

VERSE: *Remind the people to be subject to rulers and authorities, to be obedient, to [be ready to do whatever is good], to slander no one, to be peaceable and considerate, and to show true humility toward all men.* Titus 3:1,2

READING 4   BE PEACE-LOVING

READ: James 3:13-18

ANSWER: How does a person show that he/she is wise? (13) What things are earthly and unspiritual? (14-16) Describe wisdom from heaven. (17)

VERSE: *But [the wisdom that comes from heaven is first of all pure; then peace-loving,] considerate, submissive, full of mercy and good fruit, impartial and sincere.* James 3:17

SUMMARY

DISCUSS: Describe what happens when you get into an argument. What is usually the outcome?

APPLY: When you find yourself starting to argue with or complain to your parents, stop and recite Philippians 2:14-16. Thank God that He is making you blameless and pure.

BARE BASICS AND VERSE REVIEW:
           1. Avoid an argument (Prov. 20:3)
           2. Do everything without complaining or arguing (Phil. 2:14,15)
           3. Do what is good (Titus 3:1,2)
           4. Be peace-loving (James 3:17)

QUESTIONS FOR PARENTS

What do your children complain about the most? What are ways of dealing with their complaining? How do you teach children to be content? What are the causes of arguments between your children? What are the best ways of controlling arguing?

GOSSIPING

When the Jews in Thessalonica learned that Paul was preaching the word of God at Berea, they went there too, agitating the crowds and stirring them up.

Acts 17:13

GOSSIPING

INTRODUCTORY LESSON

REVIEW: What does the Bible say about arguing and complaining? (Review The Bare Basics and Key Verse.)

PRESENT: Have some of the family do a presentation on gossip and its results.

DISCUSS: What is gossip? What is the difference between exposing something wrong and gossip? Why do people gossip? Why is gossip wrong to do? When people gossip, what does that say about their hearts?

EXPLAIN: Gossips try to cause trouble and inflame situations. They want to have control over people and what they think. The Apostle Paul ran into people like that all the time as he went from place to place sharing the good news of Jesus Christ. People who didn't like what he said tried to destroy him by setting people against him.

READ: Acts 17:1-15 (Check for understanding. Clarify any difficult words or concepts.)

DISCUSS: What was Paul preaching? Why were some of the Jews upset? How did they cause trouble for Paul? Were they telling the truth about Paul? Can gossip be true? What was the problem with what they were saying?

PRAY: Ask God to show you how your words might have hurt another person. Pray that the words that come from your mouth would be wholesome and good and build others up. Pray for a pure heart and that you would not want to tear others down with the words of your mouth.

KEY VERSE:

> *Do not spread false reports.*
> *Do not help a wicked man*
> *by being a malicious witness.*
> *- Exodus 23:1*

READING 1   DON'T REPEAT STORIES

READ: Proverbs 11:13; 17:9; 18:8; 25:9-10

ANSWER: What happens when someone tells a secret? (11:13, 17:9) What do you think it means that gossip goes into a man's inmost parts? (18:8) If you reveal a secret, what happens to your reputation? (25:9-10)

VERSE: *He who covers over an offense promotes love, but [whoever repeats the matter separates close friends.]* Proverbs 17:9

READING 2   BE CAREFUL WHAT YOU SAY

READ: Matthew 12:33-37

ANSWER: Where do the things that come out of our mouth really come from? (34) What are we going to have to explain on Judgment Day? (36) Why do you think what we say is so important?

VERSE: *But I tell you that [men will have to give account on the day of judgment for every careless word they have spoken.]* Matthew 12:36

READING 3   BUILD OTHERS UP

READ: Ephesians 4:29 - 5:2

ANSWER: What kind of talk should come out of our mouths? (29) What behavior do we need to get rid of? (31)   Who do we imitate? (1)

VERSE: *[Do not let any unwholesome talk come out of your mouths,] but only what is helpful for building others up according to their needs, that it may benefit those who listen.* Ephesians 4:29

READING 4   DON'T SLANDER OTHERS

READ: James 4:11-12

ANSWER: When we speak against our brother what are we doing? (11) Who is the only One who can judge other people? (12)

VERSE: *Brothers, [do not slander one another.] Anyone who speaks against his brother or judges him speaks against the law and judges it.* James 4:11

SUMMARY

DISCUSS: How have you been hurt by someone saying something bad about you?

APPLY: Ask for forgiveness for any way that you have hurt someone by what you said about him. (Be specific if you can remember.) Watch carefully what words are coming out of your mouth.

BARE BASICS AND VERSE REVIEW:
1. Don't repeat stories (Prov. 17:9)
2. Be careful what you say (Matt. 12:36)
3. Build others up (Eph. 4:29)
4. Don't slander others (James 4:11)

QUESTIONS FOR PARENTS

What are your children hoping to gain when they talk poorly about someone else? How can you demonstrate to them the harmful effects of gossip? What are ways you can teach your children to build others up?

LYING

Peter asked her, "Tell me, is this the price you and Ananias got for the land?" "Yes," she said, "that is the price." Peter said to her, "How could you agree to test the Spirit of the Lord? Look! The feet of the men who buried your husband are at the door, and they will carry you out also."
- Acts 5:8,9

LYING

INTRODUCTORY LESSON

REVIEW: What does the Bible say about gossiping? (Review The Bare Basics and Key Verse.)

PRESENT: Have some of the family do a presentation on someone being caught-up in a lie.

DISCUSS: What is a lie? What is wrong with lying? Why do people lie? What happens to people when they lie a lot? Is there any good that comes out of lying?

EXPLAIN: When the church first started after the death and resurrection of Jesus, believers shared what they had with one another so that there weren't any people in the church who were in need. They did this out of a love for God. One couple, Ananias and Sapphira, sold some property and only gave some of the money to the church. They didn't have to give all the money to the church, but they were deceitful and lied about what they did. What happened to them shows how much God hates lying and wants His church to be pure.

READ: Acts 4:32 - 5:11 (Check for understanding. Clarify any difficult words or concepts.)

DISCUSS: Why were the believers so generous with what they owned? What was the difference between Ananias and Sapphira and the other believers who sold property? Who did the property belong to before it was sold? Could they have kept the money from the sale of the property? What was wrong with what they did? How do you know God didn't like what they did?

PRAY: Pray that God would create in you a pure heart and that you would hate lying as much as He does. Ask Him to convict you whenever you start to tell a lie. Ask Him for strength to tell the truth no matter how little the lie seems to you. Pray that He would show you how lying hurts you and separates you from Him.

KEY VERSE:

> *He who guards his lips guards his life, but*
> *he who speaks rashly will come to ruin.*
> *- Proverbs 13:3*

READING 1   GOD HATES LYING

READ: Proverbs 6:16-19; 12:22; 13:5; 19:5,9; 24:28,29

ANSWER: What are the things God hates? (6:16-19) What is wrong with
lying? What will happen to the person who lies? (19:5,9)

VERSE: *[The Lord detests lying lips,] but he delights in men who are truthful.*
Proverbs 12:22

READING 2   LYING SEPARATES US FROM GOD

READ: Isaiah 59:1-3

ANSWER: What separates us from God? (2) Will telling lies separate us from
God? (3)

VERSE: *But [your iniquities have separated you from your God;] your sins
have hidden his face from you, so that he will not hear.* Isaiah 59:2

READING 3   SATAN IS THE FATHER OF LIES

READ: John 8:42-47

ANSWER: Who is the father of lies? (44) Who always tells the truth? If you
are wise who will you listen to? If you are not listening to God, to
whom are you listening?

VERSE: *He was a murderer from the beginning, not holding to the truth, for
there is no truth in him. When he lies, he speaks his native
language, for [he is a liar and the father of lies.]* John 8:44b

READING 4   THE GREATEST LIE IS DENYING GOD

READ: Jeremiah 9:1-9

ANSWER: How does God feel about people lying and being deceitful? (1-3)
          What will He do about it? (9) What is the worst lie that people tell
          themselves? (6)

VERSE: *You live in the midst of deception; [in their deceit they refuse to
          acknowledge me, declares the Lord.]* Jeremiah 9:6

SUMMARY

DISCUSS: What is it that tempts you to lie? After you have told a lie, what
          happens?

APPLY: Confess to your parents a lie you have told them and ask for
          forgiveness. If you are tempted to lie, stop and think what the
          result will be.

BARE BASICS AND VERSE REVIEW:
          1. God hates lying (Prov. 12:22)
          2. Lying separates us from God (Isa. 59:2)
          3. Satan is the father of lies (John 8:44b)
          4. The greatest lie is denying God
                                         (Jer. 9:6)

QUESTIONS FOR PARENTS

What are your children trying to accomplish
when they lie? What is the best way for you to
react to your children's lying? How can you
teach them that lying doesn't protect them? How
can you take the incentive out of lying?

Section VI

AVOIDING
THE WAY
OF THE WICKED

BEING WICKED

Ahab said to Elijah, "So you have found me, my enemy!"
"I have found you," he answered, "because you have sold
yourself to do evil in the eyes of the Lord. I am going to bring
disaster on you. I will consume your descendants and cut off
from Ahab every last male in Israel - slave or free.'"
- I Kings 21:20,21

BEING WICKED

INTRODUCTORY LESSON

REVIEW: What does the Bible say about lying? (Review The Bare Basics and Key Verse.)

PRESENT: Have some of the family do a presentation on the actions of a wicked person.

DISCUSS: What is wickedness? Why do people choose to be wicked? What is it about evil that attracts people?

EXPLAIN: After the death of Solomon, Israel was divided into two kingdoms: the northern kingdom of Israel and the southern kingdom of Judah. Many of the kings of Judah sought the Lord and led the people in righteousness. However, the kings of Israel were wicked and did what was evil in the sight of the Lord. One of the worst kings was Ahab who was married to a very wicked woman named Jezebel. God punished Ahab and Jezebel for their evil. He also eventually punished the kingdom of Israel for its wickedness by destroying it completely.

READ: 1 Kings, Chapter 21 (Check for understanding. Clarify any difficult words or concepts.)

DISCUSS: What was the first thing that Ahab did wrong? What was Jezebel's response when Ahab was sulking because he couldn't have the vineyard? How would you describe Jezebel? What did God say about Ahab and Jezebel through Elijah the Prophet?

PRAY: Ask God to protect you from the evil of the world around you. Pray for pure hearts that would seek truth and righteousness and hate evil. Ask God to show you how destructive wickedness is.

KEY VERSE:

> *The Lord is known by his justice; the wicked*
> *are ensnared by the work of their hands.*
> *Psalm 9:16*

READING 1   THE WICKED ARE SEPARATED FROM GOD

READ: Proverbs 4:14-17; 5:22-23; 14:32; 15:26-29; 21:7

ANSWER: What path should you avoid? (4:14) Why? What does it mean that the evil deeds of a man ensnare him? (5:22) How does God view the righteous? (15:26-29)

VERSE: *[The Lord is far from the wicked] but he hears the prayers of the righteous.* Proverbs 15:29

READING 2   THE WICKED ARE QUICK TO SIN

READ: Isaiah 59:4-16

ANSWER: What can't evildoers experience? (8) Describe what our lives are like when we act in evil ways. (9-11) God doesn't like evil, but what did He do for us anyway? (16)

VERSE: *[Their feet rush into sin;] they are swift to shed innocent blood. Their thoughts are evil thoughts; ruin and destruction mark their ways.* Isaiah 59:7

READING 3   THE WICKED HATE THE LIGHT

READ: John 3:16-21

ANSWER: What happens to the person who doesn't know God? (18) Why do people like the darkness more than the light? (19) Who is the Light?

VERSE: *This is the verdict: Light has come into the world, but [men loved darkness instead of light because their deeds were evil.]* John 3:19

READING 4   THE WICKED LOVE THEMSELVES INSTEAD OF GOD

READ: 2 Timothy 3:1-9

ANSWER: Describe what people will be like in the last days. (1-5) What will
           these people oppose? (8)

VERSE: *[People will be lovers of themselves,] lovers of money, boastful, proud,
           abusive, disobedient to their parents, ungrateful, unholy, without
           love, unforgiving, slanderous, without self-control, brutal, not lovers
           of the good.* 2 Timothy 3:2,3

SUMMARY

DISCUSS: What do you think the days we are living in are like? Would you
           describe this as an age of darkness or an age of light? Why?

APPLY: Is there any type of wickedness that you are attracted to or that
           fascinates you? Confess this to God and ask that instead of evil
           being attractive to you, you would be repulsed by it.

BARE BASICS AND VERSE REVIEW:
1. The wicked are separated from God (Prov. 15:29)
2. The wicked are quick to sin (Isa. 59:7)
3. The wicked hate the light (John 3:19)
4. The wicked love themselves instead of God (2 Tim 3:2,3)

QUESTIONS FOR PARENTS

What are some ways your children show that
they are being influenced by the evil of the
world? What steps can you take to change that?
How can you show them the consequences of
wickedness?

CHEATING AND STEALING

Achan replied, "It is true! I have sinned against the Lord, the God of Israel. This is what I have done: When I saw in the plunder a beautiful robe from Babylonia, two hundred shekels of silver and a wedge of gold weighing fifty shekels, I coveted them and took them. They are hidden in the ground inside my tent, with the silver underneath."
- Joshua 7:20,21

CHEATING AND STEALING

INTRODUCTORY LESSON

REVIEW: What does the Bible say about wickedness? (Review The Bare Basics and Key Verse.)

PRESENT: Have some of the family do a presentation on what goes on in the mind of a thief planning a robbery and a student planning to cheat.

DISCUSS: What is wrong with cheating and stealing? What does cheating and stealing show about a person? What happens to a person's heart when he cheats or steals?

EXPLAIN: After having the Israelites wander around in the desert for forty years, God led them into the land He had promised them. They first destroyed the city of Jericho by the power of God without even having to fight. God had given them a command at Jericho not to keep any of the things in the city for themselves. All the plunder from the city was to be dedicated to God. A man named Achan disobeyed and brought trouble to Israel because of what he did.

READ: Joshua, Chapter 7 (Check for understanding. Clarify any difficult words or concepts.)

DISCUSS: Why did the Israelites think that they could easily defeat Ai? What happened to the Israelites because of Achan's sin? How did Joshua respond to the defeat? How did God respond to Joshua? How did Joshua find out who had brought the trouble to Israel? What had Achan done? What did the people do to Achan? Why did they have to do that? How can you tell that God hates cheating and stealing?

PRAY: Pray for hearts in your family that would be satisfied with what God has given you and would not want to get things by cheating and stealing. Pray for protection against temptation in this area. Pray for generous hearts that want to give, rather than selfish hearts that want more.

KEY VERSE:

> *Better a poor man whose walk is blameless*
> *than a rich man whose ways are perverse.*
> *Proverbs 28:6*

READING 1   GOD HATES CHEATING

READ: Proverbs 16:8; 20:23; 28:8

ANSWER: Explain 16:8 in your own words. What are differing weights and dishonest scales used for? (20:23)

VERSE: *[The Lord detests differing weights] and dishonest scales do not please him.* Proverbs 20:23

READING 2   STEALING IS SIN

READ: Leviticus 6:1-7

ANSWER: What are some ways a person can deceive his neighbor? (1-3) What does a person have to do if he deceives someone? (4,5) Will God forgive a person who cheats and steals? Under what conditions?

VERSE: *[When he thus sins and becomes guilty, he must return what he has stolen] or taken by extortion, or what was entrusted to him, or the lost property he found.* Leviticus 6:4

READING 3   A THIEF IS SEPARATED FROM GOD

READ: Zechariah 5:1-4

ANSWER: Why did God curse the land? How long do you think God's curse remains? Describe how God feels about cheating and stealing.

VERSE: *And he said to me, "This is the curse that is going out over the whole land; for according to what it says on one side, [every thief will be banished."]* Zechariah 5:3

READING 4 THE EVIL ARE KEPT OUT OF HEAVEN

READ: 1 Corinthians 6:7-11

ANSWER: Who is kept out of God's kingdom? (9) Do we do some of these
            wrong things? How are we made clean from the evil we've done?
            (11)

VERSE: *[Do you not know that the wicked will not inherit the kingdom of
            God?]* 1 Corinthians 6:9a

SUMMARY

DISCUSS: Why is cheating and stealing dishonoring to God?

APPLY: Be honest about any way you have cheated or what you have
            stolen from another person. Ask that person for forgiveness
            and return what you have stolen or make up for it in some way.

BARE BASICS AND VERSE REVIEW:
            1. God hates cheating (Prov. 20:23)
            2. Stealing is a sin (Lev. 6:4)
            3. A thief is separated from God (Zech. 5:3)
            4. The evil are kept out of heaven (1 Cor. 6:9a)

QUESTIONS FOR PARENTS

How have you seen your children cheat or steal?
What do they think they will accomplish by
cheating or stealing? How can you teach them
the bad consequences of cheating and stealing?

PLOTTING EVIL

So Haman got the robe and the horse. He robed Mordecai, and led him on horseback through the city streets, proclaiming before him, "This is what is done for the man the king delights to honor!"
- Esther 6:11

PLOTTING EVIL

INTRODUCTORY LESSON

REVIEW: What does the Bible say about cheating and stealing?   (Review The Bare Basics and Key Verse.)

PRESENT: Have some of the family do a presentation on how and why someone would plot evil.

DISCUSS: How would you define evil? Who do you think of as being evil? What are some things good people do that could be considered evil? What is the motivation behind evil?

EXPLAIN: The book of Esther is the story of how God used the Jewish queen, Esther, to deliver her people when they were about to be destroyed. The man who wanted to destroy them was named Haman, and the evil he plotted came down on him instead of the Jews. This all happened during the reign of Xerxes in Persia.

READ: Esther 3:1-11; 5:9-14; 7:1-8:2 (Check for understanding. Clarify any difficult words or concepts.)

DISCUSS: Why did Haman plot to kill the Jewish people? Why wouldn't Mordecai kneel down before Haman? Why did this upset Haman so much? How did Haman think of himself? What happened to Haman in the end? What happened to all that belonged to Haman? Why do you think things turned out the way they did?

PRAY: Pray that God would reveal any evil that you have hidden in your hearts. Pray for hearts that are free from hate and any desire to hurt someone else.

KEY VERSE:

> *Do not those who plot evil go astray?*
> *But those who plan what is good*
> *find love and faithfulness.*
> *- Proverbs 14:22*

READING 1   ONE WHO SEEKS EVIL FINDS IT

READ: Proverbs 3:29; 11:27; 17:13; 26:27; 28:10

ANSWER: What happens to the person who seeks evil? (11:27) What happens
              to those who plan good? (14:22) What does it mean to fall into
              your own pit or trap?

VERSE: *He who seeks good finds goodwill, but [evil comes to him who
              searches for it.]* Proverbs 11:27

READING 2   ONE WHO CAUSES TROUBLE WILL GET TROUBLE

READ: Psalm 7:9-16

ANSWER: What kind of judge is God? (11) What does that mean? What
              happens to the person who makes trouble? (16) Does God know
              what is in a person's heart? Will he judge that?

VERSE: *[He who digs a hole and scoops it out falls into the pit he has made.]
              The trouble he causes recoils on himself; his violence comes down on
              his own head.* Psalm 7:15,16

READING 3   DON'T PLOT EVIL

READ: Zechariah 8:14-17

ANSWER: When does God bring disaster on a people? When does He bring
              good? What are the things we need to do to experience God's
              goodness? (16,17)

VERSE: *["Do not plot evil against your neighbor,] and do not love to swear
              falsely. I hate all this," declares the Lord.* Zechariah 8:17

READING 4   GOD IS AGAINST EVIL DOERS

READ: 1 Peter 3:8-12

ANSWER: How does God command us to live? (8) How should we respond
            to evil? (9) What should we keep our mouths from doing? (10)

VERSE: *For the eyes of the Lord are on the righteous and his ears are
            attentive to their prayer, but [the face of the Lord is against those
            who do evil.]* 1 Peter 3:12

SUMMARY

DISCUSS: What are some ways you have seen where someone has fallen into
            a pit they dug? What are some examples of evil or deceit in this
            day and age? What is the outcome of this evil?

APPLY: We need to walk rightly before God. This means we should daily
            ask His Holy Spirit to show us if there is any evil or deceit in us.
            Start doing that every day.

BARE BASICS AND VERSE REVIEW:
      1. One who seeks evil finds it (Prov. 11:27)
      2. One who causes trouble will get trouble (Psa. 7:15,16)
      3. Don't plot evil (Zech 8:17)
      4. God is against evil doers (1 Pet. 3:12)

QUESTIONS FOR PARENTS

What are some examples of evil (even little
things) your children have perpetrated? How
can you help your children see that wanting evil
to happen to others will only hurt themselves?
How can you train your children to want only
good for others?

SEEKING REVENGE

"See, my father, look at this piece of your robe in my hand!
I cut off the corner of your robe but did not kill you.
Now understand and recognize that I am not guilty of
wrongdoing or rebellion. I have not wronged you, but you are
hunting me down to take my life. May the Lord judge between
you and me. And may the Lord avenge the wrongs you have
done to me, but my hand will not touch you."
- 1 Samuel 24:11,12

SEEKING REVENGE

INTRODUCTORY LESSON

REVIEW: What does the Bible say about plotting evil? (Review The Bare Basics and Key Verse.)

PRESENT: Have some of the family do a presentation on someone seeking revenge for something someone else did to them.

DISCUSS: Why do we want to "get even" with someone when they hurt us? What happens to us when we take revenge for a wrong? What happens when we forgive someone for a wrong? In whose hand should we leave the right to get even?

EXPLAIN: King Saul was chasing David and wanted to kill him. He had already attempted to kill him several times before. David was in a place where he could have easily killed Saul and taken revenge for what Saul was doing to him. Instead of hurting Saul, David showed his love for God by sparing Saul's life and doing what was right.

READ: 1 Samuel, Chapter 24 (Check for understanding. Clarify any difficult words or concepts.)

DISCUSS: Why could David have easily killed Saul? Why wouldn't David kill Saul? What did David's men want him to do? What was Saul's response to David? Do you think God wanted David to kill Saul? Why or why not? What would have happened to David if he had taken revenge against Saul?

PRAY: Pray that God would give you the strength to forgive people who hurt you rather than seek revenge. Pray for love for your enemies. Ask for forgiveness for any time you have sought revenge rather than waiting on God.

KEY VERSE:

> *Do not say,*
> *"I'll pay you back for this wrong!"*
> *Wait for the Lord, and he will deliver you.*
> *- Proverbs 20:22*

READING 1   DON'T SEEK REVENGE

READ: Proverbs 24:28,29; 25:21,22; Leviticus 19:18

ANSWER: Whose responsibility is it to repay evil? What are we to do to our enemies? (25:21) How are we to love our neighbor? (Lev. 19:18) What does that mean?

VERSE: *[Do not seek revenge or bear a grudge against one of your people,] but love your neighbor as yourself. I am the Lord.* Leviticus 19:18

READING 2   GOD KNOWS WHAT IS GOING ON

READ: Psalm 94:1-15

ANSWER: Does it sometimes seem that people who do evil aren't punished? Is God aware of everything everyone does? What will happen to all people in the end?

VERSE: *Does he who implanted the ear not hear? [Does he who formed the eye not see?]* Psalm 94:9

READING 3   DON'T PAY BACK EVIL

READ: Romans 12:17-21

ANSWER: How are we to act? (17) How do we overcome evil? (21) If we pay someone back (take revenge) what are we doing? (19)

VERSE: *[Do not repay anyone evil for evil.] Be careful to do what is right in the eyes of everybody.* Romans 12:17

READING 4   DON'T MAKE THREATS

READ: 1 Peter 2:18-25

ANSWER: When is it that we really earn God's praise? (19,20) What is Christ's example for us? (21-23)

VERSE: *When they hurled their insults at him, he did not retaliate; [when he suffered, he made no threats.]* 1 Peter 2:23

SUMMARY

DISCUSS: Have you ever been treated unfairly? How did you respond? Why is God the one who should punish evil?

APPLY: Do you feel angry at anyone now whom you would like to get back at? Confess this and pray for that person. Think of something good you can do for him/her. If you aren't angry now, remember to treat your enemy kindly when the opportunity arises.

BARE BASICS AND VERSE REVIEW:
1. Don't seek revenge (Lev. 19:18)
2. God knows what is going on (Psa. 94:9)
3. Don't pay back evil (Rom. 12:17)
4. Don't make threats (1 Pet. 2:23)

QUESTIONS FOR PARENTS

What do your children hope to accomplish by seeking revenge? What are ways you can teach your children that revenge is counterproductive? What steps can you take to train your children to forgive rather than to get even?

Section VII

FOLLOWING THE WAY OF THE RIGHTEOUS

GOODNESS AND MERCY

Her mother-in-law asked her, "Where did you glean today? Where did you work? Blessed be the man who took notice of you!" Then Ruth told her mother-in-law about the one at whose place she had been working "The name of the man I worked with today is Boaz," she said.

- Ruth 2:19

SHOWING
GOODNESS AND MERCY

INTRODUCTORY LESSON

REVIEW: What does the Bible say about seeking revenge? (Review The Bare Basics and Key Verse.)

PRESENT: Have some of the family do a presentation on how we can show mercy.

DISCUSS: What is mercy? How can we show goodness and mercy to others? How have people shown goodness and mercy to you?

EXPLAIN: The story of Ruth is a wonderful example of how doing good brings goodness to you. Ruth left her people to go back to Israel to be with and take care of her mother-in-law, Naomi. Ruth and Naomi were widows. The goodness Ruth showed to her mother-in-law was recognized by the people in the community.

READ: Ruth 2:1-23 (Check for understanding. Clarify any difficult words or concepts.)

DISCUSS: What did Boaz do for Ruth? What was Ruth's response to Boaz's kindness? What kind of man was Boaz? What was Naomi's response to what happened to Ruth?

PRAY: Pray that God would help you show greater goodness and mercy to others, starting especially with your family. Pray that He would develop in you a heart of compassion for others. Ask for forgiveness for the times you should have showed goodness or extended mercy to others and didn't.

KEY VERSE:

> *Do not withhold good from those who deserve it when it is in your power to act.*
> *- Proverbs 3:27*

READING 1 BE KIND

READ: Proverbs 3:27,28: 11:17; 12:2; 14:22,31: 22:1

ANSWER: What does verse 3:27 mean? What do those who plan good find?
(14:22) How can we honor God? (14:31)

VERSE: *He who oppresses the poor shows contempt for their Maker, but
[whoever is kind to the needy honors God.]* Proverbs 14:31

READING 2 LOVE MERCY

READ: Micah 6:8; Zechariah 7:8-10

ANSWER: What does God require of us? (Micah) What does Zechariah say
God wants us to do?

VERSE: *He has shown you, O man, what is good. And [what does the Lord
require of you? To act justly and to love mercy] and to walk humbly
with your God.* Micah 6:8

READING 3 DO GOOD

READ: Galatians 6:1-10

ANSWER: What does it mean that a man reaps what he sows? (7) Why
shouldn't we tire of doing good? (9) Who should we be especially
good to? (10)

VERSE: *[Let us not become weary in doing good,] for at the proper time we
will reap a harvest if we do not give up.* Galatians 6:9

READING 4   BE COMPASSIONATE

READ: Colossians 3:12-17

ANSWER: What kind of clothes should we put on? (12) How are we to do all things? (17)

VERSE: *Therefore, as God's chosen people, holy and dearly loved, [clothe yourselves with compassion,] kindness, humility, gentleness, and patience.* Colossians 3:12

SUMMARY

DISCUSS: What does it mean to be good to others? What is the true source of goodness?

APPLY: List some ways you could show goodness to someone this week. Do at least one of the things on your list.

BARE BASICS AND VERSE REVIEW:
    1. Be kind (Prov. 14:31)
    2. Love mercy (Micah 6:8)
    3. Do good (Gal. 6:9)
    4. Be compassionate (Col. 3:12)

QUESTIONS FOR PARENTS:

What are some areas where goodness and mercy need to be developed in your children? Where do you see them showing goodness and mercy? How can you help your children see that goodness and mercy are important qualities? How can you train them to be good and extend mercy to others?

GIVING AND BEING GENEROUS

She went away and did as Elijah had told her. So there was food every day for Elijah and for the woman and her family. For the jar of flour was not used up and the jug of oil did not run dry, in keeping with the word of the Lord spoken by Elijah.
- 1 Kings 17:15,16

GIVING AND BEING GENEROUS

INTRODUCTORY LESSON

REVIEW: What does the Bible say about goodness and mercy? (Review The Bare Basics and Key Verse.)

PRESENT: Have some of the family do a presentation on the difference between a stingy person and a generous person.

DISCUSS: What are some of the different ways people can give to other people?   How would you describe someone who is generous? Why is giving to others important? Why is giving to God important? What happens to the heart of a person who gives things away? What does the saying, "it's better to give than receive," mean?

EXPLAIN: This story takes place during the reign of the wicked king, Ahab. God sent a drought as a judgment against Israel. In difficult times God still takes care of those who love Him and give to Him. In spite of the famine in the land the widow in this story was taken care of by God. She was faithful to give and she was blessed in return.

READ: 1 Kings 17:1-16 (Check for understanding. Clarify any difficult words or concepts.)

DISCUSS: What did Elijah ask the widow to do for him? What was her response to Elijah's request? How do you think she felt about his request? How did Elijah say that God would take care of her? Did the woman have to do what Elijah asked? What would have happened if she had said that she wasn't going to share with him?

PRAY: Ask God for generous hearts that would want to give to Him in all circumstances. Ask for forgiveness for the times you knew you should have been generous and weren't. Pray that giving would be important to you and you could give with right motives and a cheerful heart.

KEY VERSE:

> *Give, and it will be given to you. A good measure, pressed down, shaken together and running over, will be poured into your lap. For with the measure you use, it will be measured to you.*
>
> *- Luke 6:38*

READING 1 REFRESH OTHERS

READ: Proverbs 3:9,10; 11:25; 19:17; 22:9; 28:27

ANSWER: Explain 3:9,10 in your own words. When we give to the poor, who are we really giving to? (19:17) If we give to the poor, what will be the result? (28:27)

VERSE: *A generous man will prosper; [he who refreshes others will himself be refreshed.]* Proverbs 11:25

READING 2 SATISFY THE NEEDS OF OTHERS

READ: Isaiah 58:3-10

ANSWER: What does fasting usually mean? More than depriving ourselves, what does God want us to do to honor Him? (6,7) If we are generous and honor God, what will be the result? (8,9) Explain verse 10 in your own words.

VERSE: *If you spend yourselves in behalf of the hungry and [satisfy the needs of the oppressed], then your light will rise in the darkness, and your night will become like the noonday.* Isaiah 58:10

READING 3 GIVE AS TO JESUS

READ: Matthew 25:31-46

ANSWER: Who will have an inheritance in the kingdom of God? (34-37) Who will be cursed? (41-43) What does Jesus mean when He says, "Whatever you did for one of the least of these brothers of mine, you did for me"? (40)

VERSE: *The King will reply, "I tell you the truth, [whatever you did for one of the least of these brothers of mine, you did for me."]* Matthew 25:40

READING 4   BE GENEROUS

READ: 2 Corinthians 9:6-15

ANSWER: Explain verse 6 in your own words. What kind of giver does God love? (7) Why does God make us rich? (11)

VERSE: *Remember this: Whoever sows sparingly will also reap sparingly, and [whoever sows generously will also reap generously.]*
2 Corinthians 9:6

SUMMARY

DISCUSS: America is much richer than the rest of the world. Do you think Christians in America give enough to God's work? Why or why not?

APPLY: Think of a way you can be generous to someone in need and do it. Also, take part of your allowance and give it to the church. (10% is a good amount.) Start doing this each week if you aren't already.

BARE BASICS AND VERSE REVIEW:
1. Refresh others (Prov. 11:25)
2. Satisfy the needs of others (Isa. 58:10)
3. Give as to Jesus (Matt. 25:40)
4. Be generous (2 Cor. 9:6)

QUESTIONS FOR PARENTS:

In what ways have you seen your children be generous? In what ways have you seen them be stingy and possessive? How can you help them see the reward of being giving and generous? What can you do to train them to be giving and generous?

WORKING HARD

From that day on, half of my men did the work, while the other half were equipped with spears, shields, bows and armor. The officers posted themselves behind all the people of Judah who were building the wall. Those who carried materials did their work with one hand and held a weapon in the other, and each of the builders wore his sword at his side as he worked. But the man who sounded the trumpet stayed with me.
- Nehemiah 4:16-18

WORKING HARD

INTRODUCTORY LESSON

REVIEW: What does the Bible say about giving and generosity? (Review The Bare Basics and Key Verse.)

PRESENT: Have some of the family do a presentation on the difference between a hardworking person and a lazy one.

DISCUSS: Why is it important to work hard? What are some things that happen to people who don't want to work? Will God reward you if you are lazy and don't do your work? What does the saying, "God helps those who help themselves," mean? God tells us to work, but can we accomplish anything of value through our own effort? Why or why not? How do we depend on God and also work hard? (See Proverbs 21:31)

EXPLAIN: After the Jews were taken to Babylon and had stayed there for seventy years they were given permission to go back and rebuild Jerusalem. God had promised this would happen. The men under Nehemiah who went to work on rebuilding the wall could have given up, as the work was hard and they faced all kinds of opposition. Because they knew God wanted them to rebuild Jerusalem, they kept working. They were diligent, and in the end they reaped a reward for their faithfulness.

READ: Nehemiah 4:1-23; 6:15,16 (Check for understanding. Clarify any difficult words or concepts.)

DISCUSS: How did their enemies try to keep the Jews from rebuilding the wall? What did the Jews have to do to continue the work? What happened to their enemies when the wall was completed?

PRAY: Pray for the strength and desire to be a faithful worker for God. Pray that you would not depend on your own strength but put your faith and trust in God. Ask God to show you any way you are lazy and dishonor Him.

KEY VERSE:

> *He who works his land will have abundant food, but the one who chases fantasies will have his fill of poverty.*
>
> *- Proverbs 28:19*

READING 1   WORK HARD

READ: Proverbs 6:6-11; 10:4,5; 12:24,27; 13:4; 14:23

ANSWER: What does the illustration of the ant mean? (6:6-8) What makes a man poor? (10:4) What brings wealth? Explain verse 14:23.

VERSE: *[All hard work brings a profit,] but mere talk leads only to poverty.* Proverbs 14:23

READING 2   DON'T BE LAZY

READ: Proverbs 19:15; 21:25,26: 24:30-34

ANSWER: What happens to the vineyard of the lazy man? (24:31) Why? What will happen to this man at harvest time?

VERSE: *Laziness brings on deep sleep, and [the shiftless man goes hungry.]* Proverbs 19:15

READING 3   WORK TO SUCCEED

READ: Ecclesiastes 11:4-6

ANSWER: If you want to succeed, what do you need to do?

VERSE: *[Sow your seed in the morning, and at evening let not your hands be idle,] for you do not know which will succeed, whether this or that, or whether both will do equally well.* Ecclesiastes 11:6

READING 4   KEEP BUSY

READ: 2 Thessalonians 3:6-14

ANSWER: In order to eat, what must a person do? (10) When people aren't busy doing work, what do they become? (11) Is God going to bless us if we don't work?

VERSE: *For even when we were with you, we gave you this rule: ["If a man will not work, he shall not eat."]* 2 Thessalonians 3:10

SUMMARY

DISCUSS: What are some of the reasons that people are poor? Laziness will make someone poor, but is laziness the cause of all poverty? What other things cause poverty?

APPLY: Think of an area in your life in which you are lazy (don't work very hard). Pray that God will strengthen you in this area and then plan what steps you can take to do better.

BARE BASICS AND VERSE REVIEW:
> 1. Work hard (Prov. 14:23)
> 2. Don't be lazy (Prov. 19:15)
> 3. Work to succeed (Ecc. 11:6)
> 4. Keep busy (2 Thess. 3:10)

QUESTIONS FOR PARENTS:

In which areas in your children's lives are they diligent and do good work? Which are areas of laziness? How can you teach them that working hard is important? What do you need to do to train them to be diligent workers?

Section VIII

APPENDICES

APPENDIX A
CRAFT and GAME IDEAS

1 DEFINING WISDOM

CRAFT: HOUSE ON A ROCK. Make a craft stick or toothpick house and glue it onto a rock or cardboard base cut to look like a rock. Put the Key Verse on a roof made out of cardboard. (APPLICATION: Remind the children that the only solid foundation to build a house on is a rock. The foundation of wisdom is the fear of the Lord and that is the rock on which to build your life.)

GAME: BUILDING RACE. Divide into teams and race to see who can build the tallest house without it falling over. Start with everyone placing a rock for the foundation, then blocks for the walls. STAND ON THE ROCK. See which team can get the most people to stand on a rock without anyone falling off. (APPLICATION: Focus on how important it is for the foundation to be solid in order to build a building that will last.)

2 BECOMING WISE

CRAFT: BIBLE MARKER. Make a Bible book marker out of paper or felt. Cut out designs to decorate with and write the Key Verse on it. Cover the paper marker with laminating paper. (APPLICATION: Since God is the giver of wisdom, and we know that we gain wisdom through the study of His Word, we want to use the Bible regularly.)

GAME: FIND IT SEARCH. Put ten things in a natural area that don't belong. Players have to really search to see the things and make a list of what they find. The one who finds the most, wins. HIDE THE VERSE. Write out the Key Verse on cards as many times as you have teams. Hide the cards. The first team to collect all the cards to make the verse, wins. Teams can exchange extra cards for missing ones. (APPLICATION: Wisdom doesn't just come to us, but it is something we really have to search for.)

3 RECOGNIZING THE WISE MAN

CRAFT: FRUIT AND VEGETABLE PRINT. Draw a fruit bowl on a piece of paper. Put fruit and vegetables in the bowl by pressing cut pieces of vegetables and fruit into an ink pad and then pressing them onto the paper. Write the Key Verse somewhere on the picture. (APPLICATION: Daniel was wise and would only eat what God wanted him to. The bowl of fruit and vegetables reminds us how obeying God shows real wisdom.)

GAME: EATING CONTEST. Without knowing what the game is about, each person picks whether to play with marshmallows or raisins. The contest is to see who can say the Key Verse with the most marshmallows or raisins in his mouth. Each player must say the verse each time a new marshmallow or raisin is added. (APPLICATION: Consider carefully before you choose anything, because choosing wisely at the beginning makes it easier to follow God later.)

4 STAYING AWAY FROM THE FOOLISH MAN

CRAFT: POTATO HEAD. Make a funky potato head to represent a foolish man by cutting out body parts from felt or construction paper and pinning them onto a potato. Make a hat with the Key Verse written on it. (APPLICATION: The person without wisdom is foolish and will do stupid things which will end up hurting him and his reputation. That person is known for a lack of good judgment.)

GAME: TREASURE HUNT. Give a difficult set of directions that the players have to follow in order to find the treasure or get to the right place. Have the treasure be a Bible or something which represents God. (APPLICATION: Remind them that a foolish man doesn't follow instructions and will end up in the wrong place.)

5 CHOOSING YOUR FRIENDS

CRAFT: COOKIES OR CANDY. Make cookies or candy to take to a family or person with whom you would like to make friends. (APPLICATION: Making friends takes effort. We can choose who we want to be friends with and then we need to make the effort to develop the friendship.)

GAME: FOLLOW THE LEADER. One player leaves the room and the others decide who the leader will be. Everyone is sitting in the circle copying whatever movement the leader does. The player comes back into the room and has to guess who the leader is. (APPLICATION: We end up being like our friends and copying their behavior.)

6 BEING A FRIEND

CRAFT: FRIENDSHIP CARD OR BRACELET. Design and make a card or friendship bracelet to give to a friend to show that friend how much you care and appreciate the friendship. (APPLICATION: To be a good friend, it is important to encourage and to show love to one another.)

GAME: PARTNER RACES. Do any kind of race that requires cooperation between two people, such as three-legged races, wheelbarrow, back-to-back, etc. (APPLICATION: The more we help one another in a friendship, the better off both people are.)

7 HONORING YOUR PARENTS

CRAFT: FAMILY PICTURE AND FRAME. Take a photo of your family or draw a picture and make a nice picture frame to go with it. (APPLICATION: Our families are a wonderful gift of God which He wants us to appreciate. He gives us our parents to learn from and tells us to honor them.)

GAME: PARENT AND CHILD RACES. Run in any race which requires a larger person and a smaller person to work together, such as races with someone on the shoulders or on the back. OBSTACLE COURSE. Have the child be blindfolded and the parent guide him/her through an obstacle course. (APPLICATION: If children learn to depend on, listen to, and trust and obey their parents they will be much better off.)

8 CONTROLLING YOUR ANGER

CRAFT: TWO-FACED MASK. Make a two-sided mask out of cardboard, a paper bag, or a paper plate. One side should be an angry face and the other a happy or contented face. The faces may be drawn or cut out and pasted on. (APPLICATION: Remind the children that they can choose whether to respond in anger or love. God did not like the face that Cain put on when he was angry.)

GAME: BALANCE BEAM PILLOW FIGHT. Teams get points by their player knocking the other player off of a 2x4 board laid on the ground with a pillow. KEEP A MAD FACE. Two players face off to see who can keep an angry face the longest. (APPLICATION: God has appropriate ways for us to respond to situations when we could get angry. Hitting and staying mad are not two of them.)

9 GIVING UP YOUR PRIDE

CRAFT: GAMES. Make a game that is difficult to play, for use at game time. You can poke two holes on the bottom edge of two cans. Loop a long string through the holes as handles to hold on to while using the cans as stilts for races. The taller the can, the more difficult to race on. Another game can be made by cutting a stick from a tree and flexible twig to make a ring, or use a dowel and a small hoop and cover them with yarn. Tie the stick to the ring with a long string. The longer the string, the harder it is. The idea is to get the ring to land on the stick when you swing it up. (APPLICATION: We tend to be proud about things that come easy to us. Everyone has things that are difficult for them and other things that are easy for them. Our talents have been given to us by God, and we should not be proud of them nor take credit for them.)

GAME: EAT HUMBLE PIE. Race to see who can eat a piece of pie the fastest with hands behind back. RELAY RACES. Race on hands and knees pushing a ball with head. Race on can stilts made in craft time. Race to see who can get ring on stick the fastest. (APPLICATION: These games can humble the best of players.)

10 OVERCOMING TEMPTATION

CRAFT: POSTER OR PLAQUE. Make a poster or design a plaque or sign to remind you not to give into temptation. Use the Key Verse in the design. COLLAGE. Make a collage of things that are tempting and cause us to take our eyes off of God. (APPLICATION: We have to be aware of our areas of weakness. We need to keep these weak. areas in mind so we can call on God for help when we face temptation.)

GAME: RED LIGHT, GREEN LIGHT. One person is the stop light. When his back is turned and he says, "green light," the other players can rush towards him. When he turns around and says, "red light," everyone must stop moving. Anyone caught moving must go back to the beginning. The first person to reach the light, wins. (APPLICATION: We are tempted to push and get away with as much as possible, but if we give into temptation we'll suffer the consequences, such as getting sent back to the start.)

11 ARGUING AND COMPLAINING

CRAFT: YARN BIG MOUTH. Draw a big mouth on some tag board. Use red yarn to fill in the lips. Put a big tongue in the mouth with the Key Verse in the middle. (APPLICATION: Our mouths get us into trouble so easily, and we need to be reminded to keep them shut.)

GAME: MOTHER MAY I? Leader gives instructions for how a player can move, making the movements as hard as possible. Before moving, a player must not complain and has to ask, "Mother, may I?" If there is any complaining or groaning or the player forgets to ask for permission, that player has to go back to the starting line. (APPLICATION: Have the children think about how they respond to requests from their mother.)

12 GOSSIPING

CRAFT: MOSAIC PICTURE. Make a mosaic picture of a fire out of little torn pieces of colored construction paper. Glue on real sticks for the wood. Write the Key Verse on the bottom. (APPLICATION: Gossip is like fire and can cause real damage unless kept under control. Remind them that without wood a fire goes out, and if people don't gossip, people don't get hurt by gossip.)

GAME: TELEPHONE. A message is written down on a piece of paper. Only the first person on each team gets to read the message. The message is passed through each team by the player receiving the message and whispering it into the next player's ear. The last person writes down the message received. Compare it to the message sent. (APPLICATION: A message gets distorted, the more people that it passes through. Don't pass on gossip.)

13 LYING

CRAFT: CRAYON RESIST. Make a design on a white paper and color it in completely with different colors of crayon. Color over that very darkly with a black crayon. Scratch a design into the black. Variations of this would be to just color the white paper with the black crayon so the design would be white or to paint black onto foil so the foil would show through when the paint is scratched. (APPLICATION: When we lie, we are trying to cover up something. At some point in time, the lie will be uncovered, and the truth will show up.)

GAME: GUESS THE TRUTH. A player makes three statements about himself, two true and one false. The others have to guess what is false. BOSSIE, BOSSIE, WHO HAS THE BELL? Players are sitting in a circle with a blind-folded person in the center. A bell is passed around the circle. When the blind fold is removed, the person in the center has to guess who has the bell behind his back. (APPLICATION: You can't always tell when someone is telling a lie. Others don't trust us after we have been caught in a lie. It is easy to deceive, but it is not right.)

14 BEING WICKED

CRAFT: STRAW CHAIN. Make a chain out of string and cut-up straws, looping the string through the straws. You can even make your own straws by rolling paper over a pencil and gluing the edge. Write the Key Verse on a paper and fasten it to the end of the chain. (APPLICATION: Evil is like chains that bind us up and are difficult to escape from.)

GAME: OBSTACLE RACE. Have teams race through an obstacle course made by running through tires, over and under benches and tables, along boards, etc. (APPLICATION: Evil will trip us up and create problems for us. Doing things God's way makes for a much smoother and safer path.)

15 CHEATING AND STEALING

CRAFT: PAPER FOLDING. Make boxes and lids out of folded paper. Origami paper is easy to use. Put the Key Verse on the lid. (APPLICATION: The empty box is a reminder of how it is better to have nothing and be right with God, than to have a lot that you have gotten by dishonest means.)

GAME: STEAL THE BACON. Form two teams. Everyone on each team is given a number. When a number is called, the players from each team with that number run out to steal the "bacon." Whoever grabs the "bacon" has to get back to his team before the other player tags him. (APPLICATION: Stealing may seem like fun and get you what you want, but at some point you will get caught.)

16 PLOTTING EVIL

CRAFT: TOOTHPICK TOWER. Make a tower out of toothpicks stuck together with little balls of playdough. (APPLICATION: The tower is a reminder that what Haman planned to do to Mordecai, ended up happening to him instead.)

GAME: HANGMAN. One player decides what word he wants the others to guess. On a chalk or dry-erase board, he marks down spaces for the letters in the word. Gallows are drawn on a board. Every time someone guesses a wrong letter, a body part is added to the person hanging from the gallows. Any time the letter is right, it is written in the correct space. The first person or team to guess the word before the person is totally hung, wins and gets the next turn to be the hangman. (APPLICATION: Evil will get its just reward in the end. It will be found out.)

17 SEEKING REVENGE

CRAFT: SPECIAL PLATE. Decorate a large paper plate with felt pens, and then paint it with shellac, to put cookies on to take to someone you have had problems with and need to forgive. (APPLICATION: It is much easier to forgive someone and overcome our desire for revenge, if we do something nice for them.)

GAME: GONNA, GONNA, GETCHYA. Have everyone sit in a large circle. The trouble-maker walks around the circle with a pillow or foam bat for a whacker. He touches the head of each player sitting down, saying, "Gonna," each time. When he wants a player to chase him, he hits that player on the head with the whacker and says, "Getchya," instead of "Gonna." He then drops the whacker and starts running. The picked player must grab the whacker and chase the trouble-maker around the circle, trying to hit him with the whacker before he gets a chance to sit down in the vacated spot. The new trouble-maker then repeats what the other trouble-maker did. (APPLICATION: We think that revenge will help the problem, but taking revenge always perpetuates the trouble.)

18 SHOWING GOODNESS AND MERCY

CRAFT: FANCY BOX OR VASE. Decorate a box to collect food and/or clothes for a family that needs help, or make a vase to take flowers to a shut-in. (APPLICATION: Goodness and mercy are actions we take that come from our love for God and desire to do his good work.)

GAME: SEARCH AND RESCUE. Divide into teams and assign each a home base. Have a number of people go out and lay down and hide. The rescuers go out and locate a hidden person. That person cannot move and must remain limp while being rescued. The rescuer must find other rescuers from his team to help carry the person back to their home base without dropping him. The team with the most rescued persons wins. (APPLICATION: We can encourage and help one another to do good works for other people. Also, we need to search for opportunities to help and serve others.)

19 GIVING AND BEING GENEROUS

CRAFT: PIGGY BANK. Make a piggy bank out of coffee can, bleach bottle, jar, etc., to start saving money to give to the church, a missionary family or someone you know of in need. (APPLICATION: Giving pleases God, and we can do it, no matter how small our income is. We need to plan to give and be generous.)

GAME: PASS THE RING. Players sit in a circle holding onto a string which has a ring on it. They move their hands continually. The player in the center of the circle tries to guess where the ring is. HOT POTATO. Players sit in a circle and toss a bean bag or tennis ball around while reciting, "One potato, two potato, three potato, four, five potato, six potato, seven potato, more. The person who ends up with the ball on "more" is out. The game continues until everyone but the winner has been eliminated. (APPLICATION: The person who holds on to material things too tightly will end up losing. The generous person will prosper.)

20 WORKING HARD

CRAFT: HAND PICTURE. Trace your hand to either make an exotic design or to fill it in with all the detail: knuckles, nails, lines, etc. Write the Key Verse on the bottom of the picture. (APPLICATION: God gave us our hands to work. We can glorify him with the work of our hands.)

GAME: WORK DETAIL. Work around the home or place where you have been meeting to clean and fix it up. (APPLICATION: When we work together, we can really accomplish a lot and also have a good time.)

APPENDIX B
ORGANIZING A FAMILY NIGHT

SEARCHING FOR TREASURE has been organized to facilitate a family night program. Family night is when families get together to learn and play together as a group rather than break off into segregated age groups as is usually the case with church programs. The focus of the program is to train fathers to be the spiritual leaders of their families by giving them teaching instruction and materials they can use in teaching their families.

Family night is broken down into three half-hour segments. During the first half-hour, the leader of the program takes the fathers as a group and teaches them the lesson they will be presenting to their families during the second half-hour. The mothers and the children work on a craft together during the time the fathers are preparing for the lesson. (See Appendix A for craft ideas.)

Three to four family units gather together during the second half-hour with the fathers sharing the teaching responsibility. The introductory lessons are used for the teaching with each father taking a part. Families or children without fathers present should be warmly included with another family. Adults and children both participate in the discussion.

During the last-half hour the fathers take the children outside or into a large room for game time. (See Appendix A for game ideas.) While the fathers and children are playing games, the mothers gather together to share ideas for applying the lesson at home with the children. The section "Questions For Parents" at the end of each chapter provides the questions for good discussion among the women.

A nursery can be made available during the family night program for children who are too young to participate in the various parts of the program. Usually children would be put in the nursery for part of, but not all, the night's activities. Some very young children are able to remain with their parents during all aspects of the program. This should be left up to the parent. Distractions can be cut down by allowing young children to color the illustration included with each lesson during the learning time.

The readings following the introductory lesson for each chapter can be used by the families as a daily study in the home. Doing the daily readings at home greatly strengthens the program.

APPENDIX C
MEMORY VERSE CARDS

These cards should be cut apart along the dotted line and kept with the study. Use them as part of a weekly review of previously memorized verses. Continue to use them for periodic review even after completing the study.

1-KV DEFINING WISDOM
PROVERBS 9:10

The fear of the Lord
is the beginning of wisdom, and
knowledge of the Holy One
is understanding.

1-1 THE FEAR OF GOD IS THE
BEGINNING OF WISDOM
PROVERBS 1:7

[The fear of the Lord is the beginning
of knowledge,] but fools despise
wisdom and discipline.

1-2 WISDOM IS PROTECTION
PROVERBS 2:12

[Wisdom will save you
from the ways of wicked men,]
from men whose words are perverse.

1-3 WISDOM IS VERY VALUABLE
PROVERBS 3:13,14

[Blessed is the man who finds wisdom,]
the man who gains understanding,
for she is more profitable than silver
and yields better returns than gold.

1-4 WISDOM IS FROM GOD
PROVERBS 8:22

[The Lord brought me forth
as the first of his works,]
before his deeds of old.

2-KV BECOMING WISE
PROVERBS 4:1

Listen, my sons,
to a father's instruction;
pay attention and gain understanding.

2-1 GOD GIVES WISDOM
PROVERBS 2:6

[For the Lord gives wisdom,
and from his mouth
come knowledge and understanding.]

2-2 TRUST GOD FOR WISDOM
PROVERBS 3:5,6

[Trust in the Lord with all your heart]
and lean not on your own
understanding; in all your ways
acknowledge him, and he will make
your paths straight.

2-3 SEEK TO GAIN WISDOM
PROVERBS 4:7

[Wisdom is supreme;
therefore get wisdom.]
Though it cost all you have,
get understanding.

2-4 BE TEACHABLE
PROVERBS 9:9

[Instruct a wise man
and he will be wiser still;]
teach a righteous man
and he will add to his learning.

3-KV RECOGNIZING THE WISE MAN
PROVERBS 14:16

A wise man fears the Lord
and shuns evil,
but a fool is hotheaded
and reckless.

3-1 A WISE MAN STANDS FIRM
PROVERBS 10:25

When the storm has swept by,
the wicked are gone, but
[the righteous stand firm forever.]

3-2 A WISE MAN LOVES DISCIPLINE
PROVERBS 12:1

[Whoever loves discipline
loves knowledge,]
but he who hates correction
is stupid.

3-3 A WISE MAN FEARS GOD
PROVERBS 14:27

[The fear of the Lord
is a fountain of life,]
turning a man from
the snares of death.

3-4 A WISE MAN LISTENS
PROVERBS 16:20

[Whoever gives heed
to instruction prospers,]
and blessed is he
who trusts in the Lord.

4-KV STAYING AWAY FROM THE
FOOLISH MAN
PROVERBS 10:23

A fool finds pleasure in evil conduct,
but a man of understanding
delights in wisdom.

4-1 A FOOL WILL BE DESTROYED
PROVERBS 1:32

For
[the waywardness of the simple
will kill them,]
and the complacency of fools
will destroy them.

4-2 A WICKED MAN WILL GET CAUGHT
PROVERBS 5:22

[The evil deeds of a wicked man
ensnare him;]
the cords of his sin
hold him fast.

4-3 A FOOL WILL BE PUNISHED
PROVERBS 10:13

Wisdom is found on the lips
of the discerning, but
[a rod is for the back of him
who lacks judgment.]

4-4 A FOOL HATES INSTRUCTION
AND HIMSELF
PROVERBS 15:32

[He who ignores discipline
despises himself,]
but whoever heeds correction
gains understanding.

5-KV CHOOSING YOUR FRIENDS
2 CORINTHIANS 6:15

What harmony is there between
Christ and Belial?
What does a believer have in common
with an unbeliever?

5-1 YOU BECOME LIKE YOUR FRIENDS
PROVERBS 13:20

[He who walks with the wise
grows wise,
but a companion of fools
suffers harm.]

5-2 BAD FRIENDS HURT
YOUR CHARACTER
1 CORINTHIANS 15:33
Do not be misled:
["Bad company
corrupts good character."]

5-3 DON'T BE YOKED
WITH UNBELIEVERS
2 CORINTHIANS 6:14

[Do not be yoked together with
unbelievers.] For what do righteousness
and wickedness have in common?
Or what fellowship can light have
with darkness?

5-4 DON'T ASSOCIATE WITH
EVIL PEOPLE
EPHESIANS 5:11

[Have nothing to do
with the fruitless deeds of darkness,]
but rather expose them.

6-KV BEING A FRIEND
PROVERBS 17:17

A friend loves at all times,
and a brother is born
for adversity.

6-1 A FRIEND CAN BE TRUSTED
PROVERBS 27:6

[Wounds from a friend
can be trusted,]
but an enemy
multiplies kisses.

6-2 A FRIEND IS HELPFUL
ECCLESIASTES 4:10

[If one falls down,
his friend can help him up.]
But pity the man who falls
and has no one to help him up.

6-3 A FRIEND MAKES SACRIFICES
JOHN 15:13

[Greater love has no man than this,
that he lay down his life for his friends.]

6-4 A FRIEND SHOWS LOVE
ROMANS 13:10

[Love does no harm to its neighbor.]
Therefore love is
the fulfillment of the law.

7-KV HONORING YOUR PARENTS
PROVERBS 30:17

The eye that mocks a father,
that scorns obedience to a mother,
will be pecked out by the ravens of the
valley, will be eaten by the vultures.

7-1 LISTEN TO YOUR PARENTS
PROVERBS 6:20

My son,
[keep your father's commands]
and do not forsake
your mother's teaching.

7-2 HONOR YOUR PARENTS
EXODUS 20:12

[Honor your father and your mother,]
so that you may live long in the land
the Lord your God is giving you.

7-3 OBEY YOUR PARENTS IN THE LORD
EPHESIANS 6:1
[Children, obey your parents in the Lord,]
for this is right.

7-4 OBEY YOUR PARENTS
IN EVERYTHING
COLOSSIANS 3:20

[Children, obey your parents in everything,]
for this pleases the Lord.

8-KV CONTROLLING YOUR ANGER
PROVERBS 15:1

A gentle answer turns away wrath,
but a harsh word stirs up anger.

8-1 A WISE MAN AVOIDS ANGER
PROVERBS 12:16

A fool shows his annoyance at once,
but [a prudent man overlooks an insult.]

8-2 AN ANGRY MAN WILL SIN
PROVERBS 29:22

[An angry man stirs up dissension,]
and a hot-tempered one
commits many sins.

8-3 GOD JUDGES OUR ANGER
MATTHEW 5:22a

But I tell you that
[anyone who is angry with his brother
will be subject to judgment.]

8-4 ANGER DOES NOT HONOR GOD
JAMES 1:19,20

Everyone should be quick to listen,
slow to speak,
and slow to become angry, for
[man's anger does not bring about
the righteous life that God desires.]

9-KV GIVING UP YOUR PRIDE
ISAIAH 2:11

The eyes of the arrogant man
will be humbled
and the pride of men
brought low; the Lord alone
will be exalted in that day.

9-1 A PRIDEFUL PERSON WILL FALL
PROVERBS 16:18

[Pride goes before destruction,]
and a haughty spirit before a fall.

9-2 GOOD THINGS COME FROM GOD
DEUTERONOMY 8:10

When you have eaten and are satisfied,
[praise the Lord your God
for the good land he has given you.]

9-3 DON'T TRUST IN YOURSELF
ISAIAH 2:22

[Stop trusting in man,]
who has but a breath in his nostrils.
Of what account is he?

9-4 THE PROUD WILL BE HUMBLED
MATTHEW 23:12

For
[whoever exalts himself will be humbled,]
and whoever humbles himself
will be exalted.

10-KV OVERCOMING TEMPTATION
HEBREWS 4:15

For we do not have a high priest
who is unable to sympathize
with our weaknesses, but we have one
who was tempted in every way,
just as we are - yet without sin.

10-1 DO NOT GIVE INTO SIN
PROVERBS 1:10

My son,
[if sinners entice you,
do not give into them.]

10-2 GOD WILL HELP YOU OVERCOME TEMPTATION
1 COR. 10:13

No temptation has seized you except what is common to man. And [God is faithful; he will not let you be tempted beyond what you can bear.] But when you are tempted, he will also provide a way out so that you can stand up under it.

10-3 GOD UNDERSTANDS OUR NEEDS
HEBREWS 4:16

[Let us then approach the throne of grace with confidence, so that we may receive mercy and find grace to help us in our time of need.]

10-4 GOD DOES NOT TEMPT US
JAMES 1:13

When tempted, no one should say, "God is tempting me." For [God cannot be tempted by evil, nor does he tempt anyone.]

11-KV ARGUING AND COMPLAINING
PROVERBS 18:6

A fool's lips bring him strife, and his mouth invites a beating.

11-1 AVOID AN ARGUMENT
PROVERBS 20:3

[It is to a man's honor to avoid strife,] but every fool is quick to quarrel.

11-2 DO EVERYTHING WITHOUT COMPLAINING OR ARGUING
PHILIPPIANS 2:14,15

[Do everything without complaining or arguing,] so that you may become blameless and pure, children of God without fault in a crooked and depraved generation.

11-3 DO WHAT IS GOOD
TITUS 3:1,2

Remind the people to be subject to rulers and authorities, to be obedient, to [be ready to do whatever is good,] to slander no one, to be peaceable and considerate, and to show true humility toward all men.

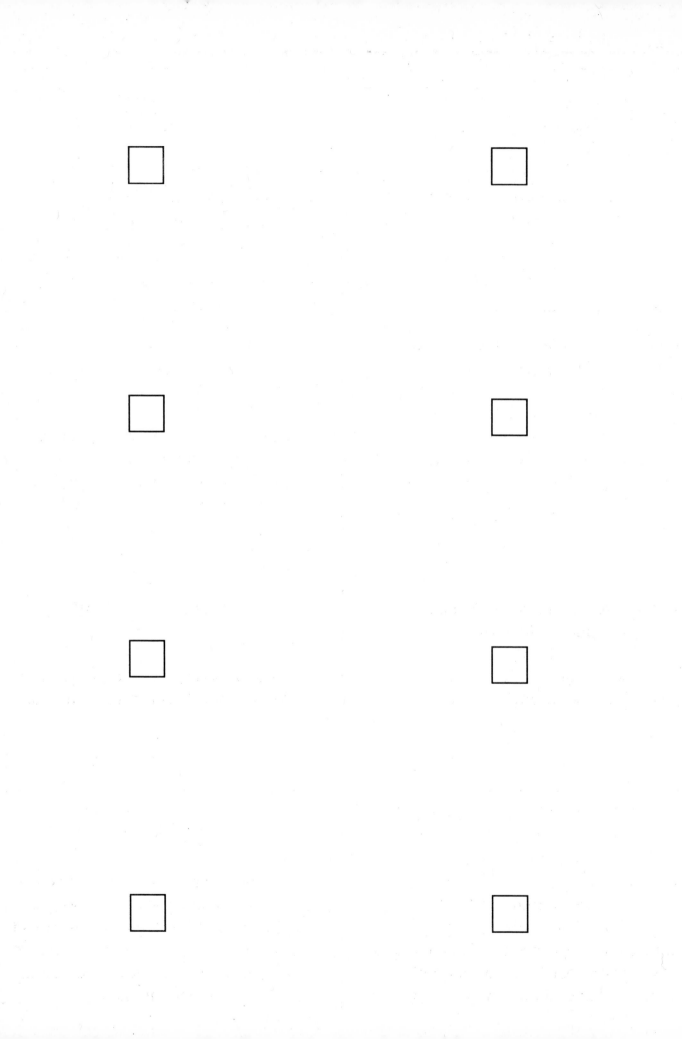

11-4 BE PEACE-LOVING
JAMES 3:17

But [the wisdom that comes from heaven is first of all pure; then peace-loving,] considerate, submissive, full of mercy and good fruit, impartial and sincere.

12-KV GOSSIPING
EXODUS 23:1

Do not spread false reports. Do not help a wicked man by being a malicious witness.

12-1 DON'T REPEAT STORIES
PROVERBS 17:9

He who covers over an offense promotes love, but [whoever repeats the matter separates close friends.]

12-2 BE CAREFUL WHAT YOU SAY
MATTHEW 12:36

But I tell you that [men will have to give account on the day of judgment for every careless word they have spoken.]

12-3 BUILD OTHERS UP
EPHESIANS 4:29

[Do not let any unwholesome talk come out of your mouths,] but only what is helpful for building others up according to their needs, that it may benefit those who listen.

12-4 DON'T SLANDER OTHERS
JAMES 4:11

Brothers, [do not slander one another.] Anyone who speaks against his brother or judges him speaks against the law and judges it.

13-KV LYING
PROVERBS 13:3

He who guards his lips guards his life, but he who speaks rashly will come to ruin.

13-1 GOD HATES LYING
PROVERBS 12:22

[The Lord detests lying lips,] but he delights in men who are truthful.

13-2 LYING SEPARATES US FROM GOD
ISAIAH 59:2

But
[your iniquities have separated
you from your God;]
your sins have hidden his face
from you, so that he will not hear.

13-3 SATAN IS THE FATHER OF LIES
JOHN 8:44b

He was a murderer from the beginning,
not holding to the truth, for there is no
truth in him. When he lies, he speaks
his native language, for
[he is a liar and the father of lies.]

13-4 THE GREATEST LIE IS DENYING GOD
JEREMIAH 9:6

You live in the midst of deception;
[in their deceit they refuse to
acknowledge me, declares the Lord.]

14-KV BEING WICKED
PSALM 9:16

The Lord is known by his justice;
the wicked are ensnared by the work
of their hands.

14-1 THE WICKED ARE SEPARATED FROM GOD
PROVERBS 15:29

[The Lord is far from the wicked]
but he hears the prayers
of the righteous.

14-2 THE WICKED ARE QUICK TO SIN
ISAIAH 59:7

[Their feet rush into sin;]
they are swift to shed innocent blood.
Their thoughts are evil thoughts;
ruin and destruction mark their ways.

14-3 THE WICKED HATE THE LIGHT
JOHN 3:19

This is the verdict:
Light has come into the world, but
[men loved darkness instead of light
because their deeds were evil.]

14-4 THE WICKED LOVE THEMSELVES INSTEAD OF GOD
2 TIMOTHY 3:2,3

[People will be lovers of themselves,]
lovers of money, boastful, proud, abusive,
disobedient to their parents, ungrateful,
unholy, without love, unforgiving,
slanderous, without self-control, brutal, not
lovers of the good.

15-KV CHEATING AND STEALING
PROVERBS 28:6

Better a poor man whose
walk is blameless
than a rich man
whose ways are perverse.

15-1 GOD HATES CHEATING
PROVERBS 20:23

[The Lord detests differing weights,]
and dishonest scales
do not please him.

15-2 STEALING IS SIN
LEVITICUS 6:4

[When he thus sins and becomes guilty,
he must return what he has stolen] or
taken by extortion, or what was
entrusted to him, or the lost property
he found.

15-3 A THIEF IS SEPARATED FROM GOD
ZECHARIAH 5:3

And he said to me, "This is the curse
that is going out over the whole land;
for according to what it says on one side,
[every thief will be banished."]

15-4 THE EVIL ARE KEPT
OUT OF HEAVEN
1 CORINTHIANS 6:9a

[Do you not know that the wicked
will not inherit the kingdom of God?]

16-KV PLOTTING EVIL
PROVERBS 14:22

Do not those who plot evil go astray?
But those who plan what is good
find love and faithfulness.

16-1 ONE WHO SEEKS EVIL FINDS IT
PROVERBS 11:27

He who seeks good finds goodwill,
but
[evil comes to him who searches for it.]

16-2 ONE WHO CAUSES TROUBLE
WILL GET TROUBLE
PSALM 7:15,16

[He who digs a hole and scoops it out
falls into the pit he has made.]
The trouble he causes recoils on himself;
his violence comes down
on his own head.

16-3 DON'T PLOT EVIL
ZECHARIAH 8:17

["Do not plot evil against your neighbor,]
and do not love to swear falsely.
I hate all this," declares the Lord.

16-4 GOD IS AGAINST EVIL DOERS
1 PETER 3:12

For the eyes of the Lord
are on the righteous and his ears are
attentive to their prayer, but
[the face of the Lord is against
those who do evil.]

17-KV SEEKING REVENGE
PROVERBS 20:22

Do not say,
"I'll pay you back for this wrong!"
Wait for the Lord,
and he will deliver you.

17-1 DON'T SEEK REVENGE
LEVITICUS 19:18

[Do not seek revenge or bear a grudge
against one of your people,]
but love your neighbor as yourself.
I am the Lord.

17-2 GOD KNOWS WHAT IS GOING ON
PSALM 94:9

Does he who implanted the ear not hear?
[Does he who formed the eye not see?]

17-3 DON'T PAY BACK EVIL
ROMANS 12:17

[Do not repay anyone evil for evil.]
Be careful to do what is right
in the eyes of everybody.

17-4 DON'T MAKE THREATS
1 PETER 2:23

When they hurled their insults at him,
he did not retaliate;
[when he suffered, he made no threats.]

18-KV SHOWING GOODNESS
AND MERCY
PROVERBS 3:27

Do not withhold good
from those who deserve it,
when it is in your power to act.

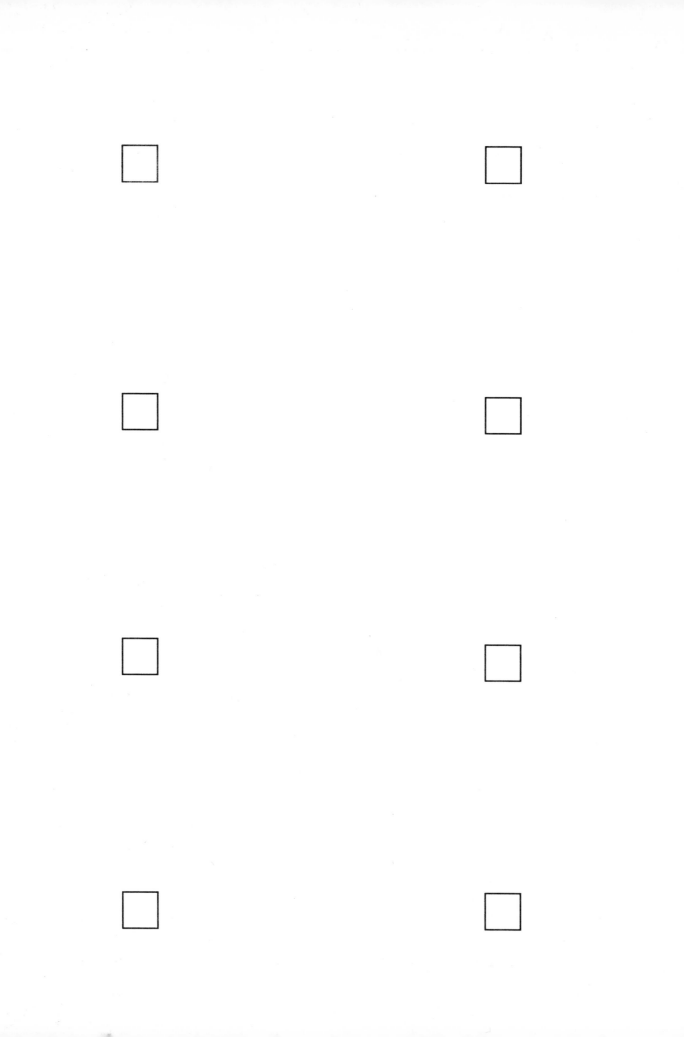

18-1 BE KIND
PROVERBS 14:31

He who oppresses the poor
shows contempt for their Maker, but
[whoever is kind to the needy
honors God.]

18-2 LOVE MERCY
MICAH 6:8

He has shown you,
O man, what is good. And
[what does the Lord require of you?
To act justly and to love mercy]
and to walk humbly with your God.

18-3 DO GOOD
GALATIANS 6:9

[Let us not become weary
in doing good,]
for at the proper time
we will reap a harvest
if we do not give up.

18-4 BE COMPASSIONATE
COLOSSIANS 3:12

Therefore as God's chosen people,
holy and dearly loved,
[clothe yourselves with compassion,]
kindness, humility, gentleness,
and patience.

19-KV GIVING AND BEING GENEROUS
LUKE 6:38

Give, and it will be given to you.
A good measure, pressed down, shaken
together and running over, will be poured
into your lap. For with the measure you
use, it will be measured to you.

19-1 REFRESH OTHERS
PROVERBS 11:25

A generous man will prosper;
[he who refreshes others
will himself be refreshed.]

19-2 SATISFY THE NEEDS OF OTHERS
ISAIAH 58:10

If you spend yourselves
in behalf of the hungry and
[satisfy the needs of the oppressed,]
then your light will rise in the darkness,
and your night will become like the noonday.

19-3 GIVE AS TO JESUS
MATTHEW 25:40

The King will reply, "I tell you the truth,
[whatever you did for one of the least of
these brothers of mine, you did for me."]

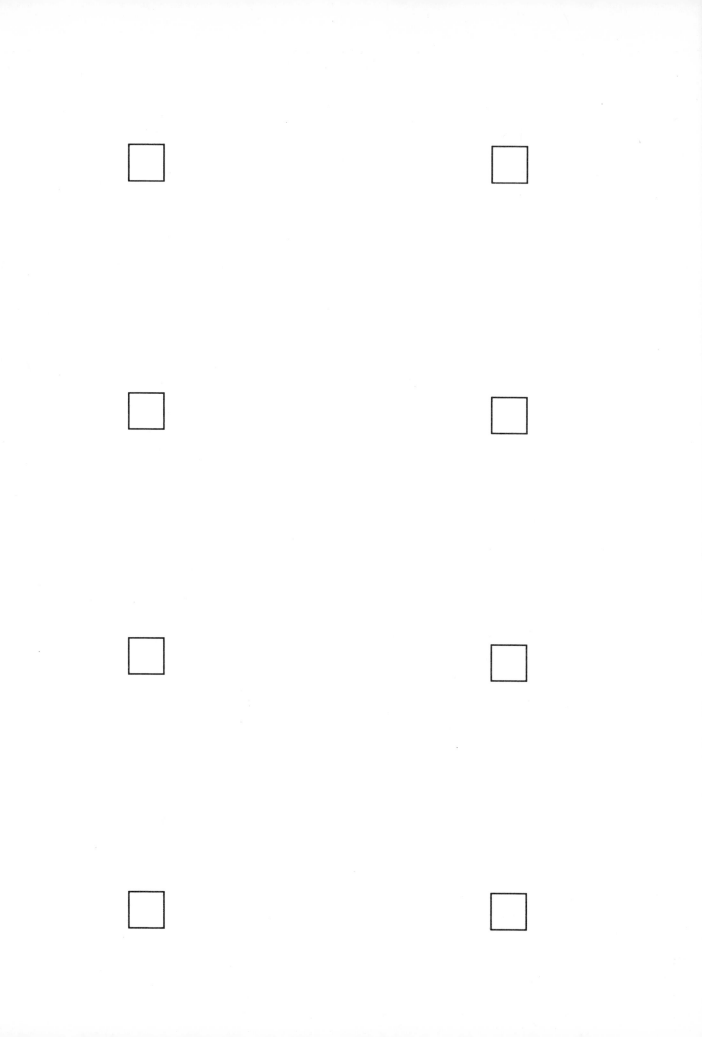

19-4 BE GENEROUS
2 CORINTHIANS 9:6

Remember this:
Whoever sows sparingly
will also reap sparingly, and
[whoever sows generously
will also reap generously.]

20-KV WORKING HARD
PROVERBS 28:19

He who works his land
will have abundant food,
but the one who chases fantasies
will have his fill of poverty.

20-1 WORK HARD
PROVERBS 14:23

[All hard work brings a profit,]
but mere talk leads only to poverty.

20-2 DON'T BE LAZY
PROVERBS 19:15

Laziness brings on deep sleep,
and [the shiftless man goes hungry.]

20-3 WORK TO SUCCEED
ECCLESIASTES 11:6

[Sow your seed in the morning, and at
evening let not your hands be idle,]
for you do not know which will
succeed, whether this or that, or
whether both will do equally well.

20-4 KEEP BUSY
2 THESSALONIANS 3:10

For even when we were with you
we gave you this rule:
["If a man will not work,
he shall not eat."]

APPENDIX D

THE GAME

PUTTING THE GAME TOGETHER

The game board is designed to be cut out of this book and taped together. The family can color it and then cover it with clear contact paper to protect it. The squares on the board should be colored in six different colors, such as red, orange, yellow, green, blue, purple. The order of colors should remain the same over the whole board. The squares with a written instruction should be left blank.

The card sheets should be cut apart and the cards stored in an envelope. The Key Verse sheet should not be cut apart, as this is a reference sheet.

You will need to make extra copies of the Treasure Sheet or figure out some other way to keep track of the Key Verses recited. The copies of the Treasure Sheet will need to be cut apart so each player can have one small Treasure Sheet to fill up.

For markers you can use coins, buttons, etc. or design and make your own. You will also need a die to play the game.

GAME RULES

PLAYERS: Two or more can play. All ages can play if played as a family, otherwise the players must be able to read.

OBJECT: The object of the game is to be the first to reach the SPRING OF WISDOM with a full load of treasure.

TO PLAY:

1. TO START: Each player takes a turn rolling the die. The player with the highest roll goes first. Play moves clockwise from the first player. Each player must start by the camel at the place marked, "Your journey begins here."

2. TO MOVE: A player rolls one die and moves the number of spaces shown. Upon landing on a square, a player draws a card and then follows the instructions on the card. If a player lands on a "BAD RESPONSE" (i.e., "You are full of pride") space then the player must roll a 3 to get off. If a player lands on a "GOOD RESPONSE" (i.e., "You worked hard") space then the player may take the short cut.

3. USE OF CARDS: A player must use the card drawn at the player's predetermined level of play (see LEVEL OF PLAY) and follow the instructions on the card. The verse on the "You Remember" cards must be recited, repeated or read before a player can try for a Key Verse or move ahead to the next space of the same color. A player can either try for the Key Verse or move ahead but, not do both. The verse on the "You Forgot" cards must be recited, repeated, or read, or a player will have to go back to the space he/she was on before rolling the die.

4. FILLING UP THE TREASURE SHEET: When a player has a "You Remember" card, the player can try for a Key Verse. The player can ask for a topic hint (the Bare Basic) for whatever number the player wishes to fill on the Treasure Sheet. Whoever is the "Keeper of the Treasure" (has the Key Verse reference sheet) then reads the topic. Example: the player asks for number 1 so the Keeper says, "Defining Wisdom, Proverbs 9:10". The player must then be able to recite that verse from memory. If the player recites the verse, then the player can mark off the appropriate spot on the Treasure Sheet.

    NOTE: Only the Key Verses that have already been memorized in the study have to be recited to consider the Treasure Sheet full. In other words, if you have only worked through chapters one through four of *Searching for Treasure,* then only numbers 1, 2, 3, and 4 would need to be filled on the Treasure Sheet. As you work through the study, you can choose which sections to fill on the sheet. The game can get too long for some children if too many verses are required for a "full" load of treasure. Circle the numbers on the Treasure Sheet that will need to be filled for that game.

5. LEVELS OF PLAY:

LEVEL ONE: For this level of play, a player must only read what is written on the card. Non-readers may repeat back either the verse or the Bare Basic after it has been read. NOTE: This is the level of play for everyone on cards where the verses have not yet been memorized or for players who are not using the study. The cards have a square on the back. Fill in this square once the verse on the card has been memorized. That way the card can either be picked up and read by the player (if the verse has not yet been memorized) or given to another player (if the verse has been memorized) who will read the question aloud so the player whose turn it is cannot cheat by looking at the verse written on the card.

LEVEL TWO: At this level of play, the player must be able to recite from memory the part of the verse between the [ ] marks. This is all that is required of younger children, who only memorize that part of the verse while doing the study.

LEVEL THREE: For advanced play the player must be able to recite the entire verse from memory.

NOTE: So that an entire family can play together and be sufficiently challenged, different players can be playing on different levels.

TO WIN:

The first player to land at the "SPRING OF WISDOM" with a full load of treasure, wins. No one can land on the spring until his/her Treasure Sheet is full. Players will have to wait on the space just before the spring to fill up their sheets. Once a player reaches this space, the player may choose a Key Verse to say each time it is his/her turn until the Treasure Sheet is full, at which time the player can land on the SPRING OF WISDOM. Play can continue with the remaining players even after one person has arrived at the SPRING OF WISDOM and has won the game.

GAME CARDS

These cards should be cut apart along the dotted line and stored with the game board. When the verse on the card has been memorized as part of the study, fill in the square on the back.

For more information: In the instructions see note under level of play — level one of game.

-1   You looked to the world for wisdom. You believed men are the source of all knowledge. You forgot PROVERBS 1:7, THE FEAR OF GOD IS THE BEGINNING OF WISDOM. Say verse or go back.

[The fear of the Lord is the beginning of knowledge,] but fools despise wisdom and discipline.

1-2   Someone tries to get you to change your beliefs by distorting the truth. You remember PROVERBS 2:12, WISDOM IS PROTECTION. Say verse to move ahead or try for Key Verse.

[Wisdom will save you from the ways of wicked men,] from men whose words are perverse.

-3   You started chasing after the riches of the world, thinking that money is more important than wisdom. You forgot PROVERBS 3:13,14, WISDOM IS VERY VALUABLE. Say verse or go back.

[Blessed is the man who finds wisdom,] the man who gains understanding, for she is more profitable than silver and yields better returns than gold.

1-4   Someone questions you about the origin of wisdom. You know that wisdom has always existed. You remember PROVERBS 8:22, WISDOM IS FROM GOD. Say verse to move ahead or try for Key Verse.

[The Lord brought me forth as the first of his works,] before his deeds of old.

2-1   You are reading all kinds of self-help books but not the Bible. You'll never be wise. You forgot PROVERBS 2:6, GOD GIVES WISDOM. Say verse or go back.

[For the Lord gives wisdom, and from his mouth come knowledge and understanding.]

2-2   You have a difficult decision to make, but you can make a wise one. You remember PROVERBS 3:5,6, TRUST GOD FOR WISDOM. Say verse to move ahead or try for Key Verse.

[Trust in the Lord with all your heart] and lean not on your own understanding; in all your ways acknowledge him, and he will make your paths straight.

-3   You want to become wise so you start studying your Bible. You remember PROVERBS 4:7, SEEK TO GAIN WISDOM. Say verse to move ahead or try for Key Verse.

Wisdom is supreme; therefore get wisdom.]
Though it cost all you have,
get understanding.

2-4   You wouldn't listen to good advice and went your own way. You forgot PROVERBS 9:9, BE TEACHABLE. Say verse or go back.

[Instruct a wise man
and he will be wiser still;]
teach a righteous man and
he will add to his learning.

-1   You get caught up listening to people who hate God's truth and find yourself doubting God. You forgot PROVERBS 10:25, A WISE MAN STANDS FIRM. Say verse or go back.

When the storm has swept by,
the wicked are gone, but
[the righteous stand firm forever.]

3-2   You are disciplined and get angry instead of learning from your trouble and seeking God. You forgot PROVERBS 12:1, A WISE MAN LOVES DISCIPLINE. Say verse or go back.

[Whoever loves discipline loves knowledge,]
but he who hates correction is stupid.

3-3   As you read God's word your love for Him increases. You remember PROVERBS 14:27, A WISE MAN FEARS GOD. Say verse to go ahead or try for Key Verse.

[The fear of the Lord is a fountain of life,]
turning a man from the snares of death.

3-4   You pay attention to what your parents have to say and want to learn. You remember PROVERBS 16:20, A WISE MAN LISTENS. Say verse to go ahead or try for Key Verse.

Whoever gives heed to instruction prospers,
and [blessed is he who trusts in the Lord.]

4-1   Some friends try to get you involved in doing something where you could get hurt. You tell them you won't do it. You remember PROVERBS 1:32, A FOOL WILL BE DESTROYED. Say verse to move ahead or try for Key Verse.

For [the waywardness of the simple
will kill them,]
and the complacency of fools will destroy them.

4-2   You plan on doing something wrong, but then you stop yourself. You remember PROVERBS 5:22, A WICKED MAN WILL GET CAUGHT. Say verse to move ahead or try for Key Verse.

[The evil deeds of a wicked man ensnare
him;] the cords of his sin hold him fast.

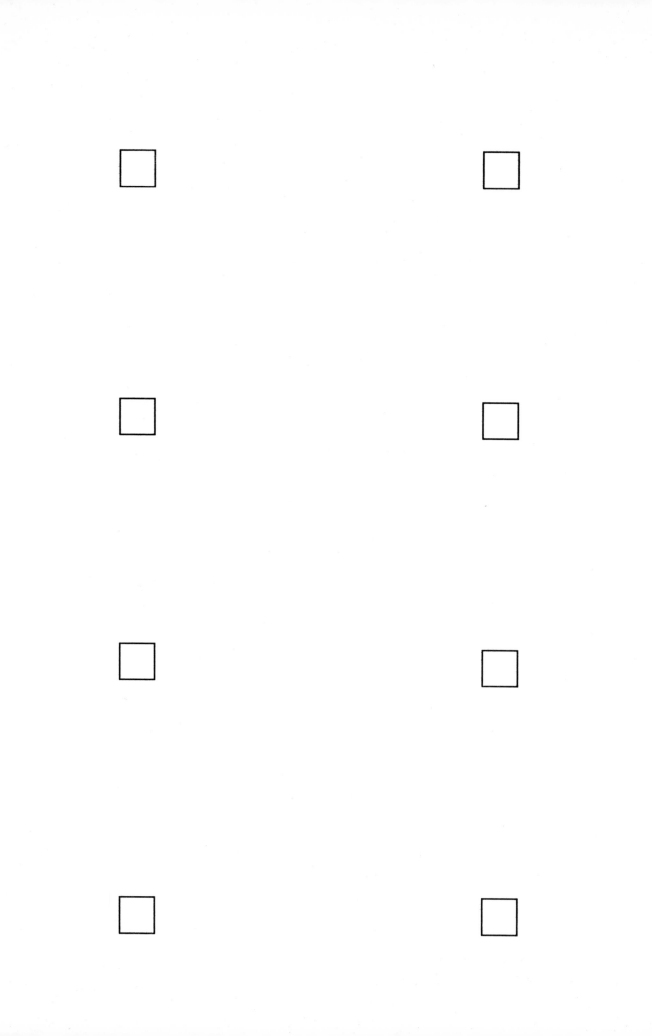

-3   Instead of following God's rules, you think you'll do things your way. You find yourself in real trouble. You forgot PROVERBS 10:13, A FOOL WILL BE PUNISHED. Say verse or go back.

Wisdom is found on the lips of the discerning, but [a rod is for the back of him who lacks judgment.]

4-4   You get mad every time someone tries to correct your mistakes. You are being a fool. You forgot PROVERBS 15:32, A FOOL HATES INSTRUCTION AND HIMSELF. Say verse or go back.

[He who ignores discipline despises himself,] but whoever heeds correction gains understanding.

-1   You see a boy who is obedient to his parents, a good student, and a hard worker. You want him for your friend. You remember PROVERBS 13:20, YOU BECOME LIKE YOUR FRIENDS. Say verse to move ahead or try for Key Verse.

[He who walks with the wise grows wise, but a companion of fools suffers harm.]

5-2   You get caught with some kids throwing rocks at windows. Your parents are upset. You forgot 1 CORINTHIANS 15:33, BAD FRIENDS HURT YOUR CHARACTER. Say verse or go back.

Do not be misled: ["Bad·company corrupts good character."]

-3   You are starting to date and sort of like someone who isn't a Christian. You decide not to go out. You remember 2 CORINTHIANS 6:14, DON'T BE YOKED WITH UNBELIEVERS. Say verse to move ahead or try for Key Verse.

[Do not be yoked together with unbelievers.] For what do righteousness and wickedness have in common? Or what fellowship can light have with darkness?

5-4   You know a kid steals and cheats, but you want to be his friend anyway. You forgot EPHESIANS 5:11, DON'T ASSOCIATE WITH EVIL PEOPLE.
Say verse or go back.

[Have nothing to do with the fruitless deeds of darkness,] but rather expose them.

5-1   Your best friend tells you that you're not being very nice. You listen to what she says. You remember PROVERBS 27:6, A FRIEND CAN BE TRUSTED. Say verse to move ahead or try for Key Verse.

[Wounds from a friend can be trusted,] but an enemy multiplies kisses.

6-2   Everyone is ganging up on your friend and you go to his defense. You remember ECCLESIASTES 4:10, A FRIEND IS HELPFUL. Say verse to move ahead or try for Key Verse.

[If one falls down, his friend can help him up.] But pity the man who falls and has no one to help him up.

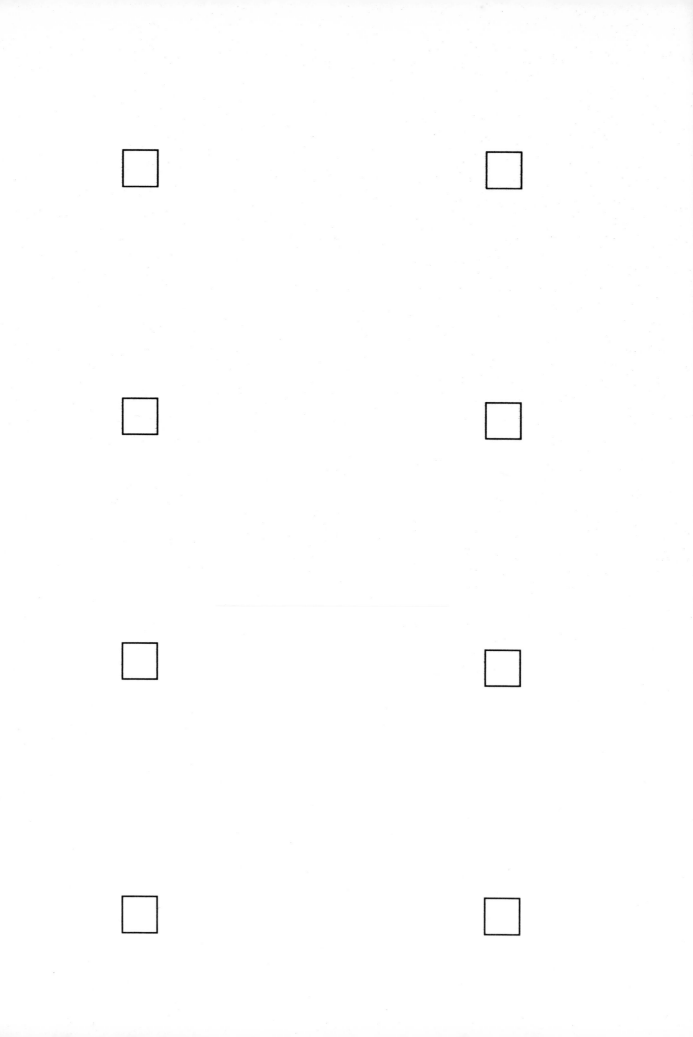

-3 Your friend really needs your help on a project, but you want to go swimming instead. You forgot JOHN 15:13, A FRIEND MAKES SACRIFICES. Say verse or go back.

Greater love has no man than this, that he lay down his life for his friends.]

6-4 You are good to your friend to her face, but you talk about her behind her back. You forgot ROMANS 13:10, A FRIEND SHOWS LOVE. Say verse or go back.

[Love does no harm to its neighbor.] Therefore love is the fulfillment of the law.

-1 Your dad has told you not to hang around with certain kids. You avoid those kids. You remember PROVERBS 6:20, LISTEN TO YOUR PARENTS. Say verse to move ahead or try for Key Verse.

My son, [keep your father's commands] and do not forsake your mother's teaching.

7-2 Everyone is talking about their parents, and you criticize yours too. You forgot EXODUS 20:12, HONOR YOUR PARENTS. Say verse or go back.

[Honor your father and your mother,] so that you may live long in the land the Lord your God is giving you.

-3 You were told to clean your room. You did it even though you wanted to go bike riding. You remember EPHESIANS 6:1, OBEY YOUR PARENTS IN THE LORD. Say verse to move ahead or try for Key Verse.

[Children, obey your parents in the Lord,] for this is right.

7-4 Your parents tell you to go straight home from the game but you mess around instead. You forgot COLOSSIANS 3:20, OBEY YOUR PARENTS IN EVERYTHING. Say verse or go back.

[Children, obey your parents in everything,] for this pleases the Lord.

-1 A friend calls you a name so you punch him in the nose. You forgot PROVERBS 12:16, A WISE MAN AVOIDS ANGER. Say verse or go back.

[A fool shows his annoyance at once,] but a prudent man overlooks an insult.

8-2 When you got pushed out of line, you pushed back and knocked someone down. You forgot PROVERBS 29:22, AN ANGRY MAN WILL SIN. Say verse or go back.

[An angry man stirs up dissension,] and a hot-tempered one commits many sins.

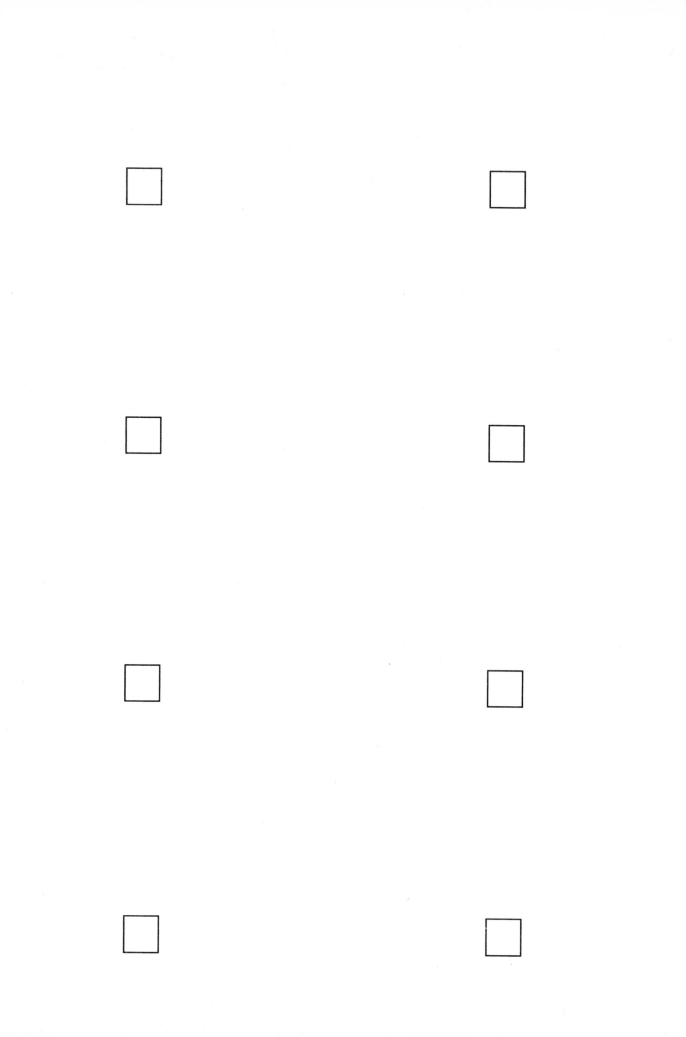

-3 You could have gotten angry when your brother lost your favorite toy but you didn't. You remember MATTHEW 5:22a, GOD JUDGES OUR ANGER. Say verse to move ahead or try for Key Verse.

But I tell you that [anyone who is angry with his brother will be subject to judgment.]

8-4 You could have gotten angry when you got thrown out of the game unfairly, but you didn't. You remember JAMES 1:19,20, ANGER DOES NOT HONOR GOD. Say verse to move ahead or try for Key Verse.

Everyone should be quick to listen, slow to speak, and slow to become angry, for [man's anger does not bring about the righteous life that God desires.]

-1 You are amused at the baby who is so proud of his first steps. You remember PROVERBS 16:18, A PRIDEFUL PERSON WILL FALL. Say verse to move ahead or try for Key Verse.

[Pride goes before destruction,] and a haughty spirit before a fall.

9-2 People comment on your great work. You appreciate the praise, but you give the thanks to God for the gifts he has given you. You remember DEUTERONOMY 8:10, GOOD THINGS COME FROM GOD. Say verse to move ahead or try for Key Verse.

When you have eaten and are satisfied, [praise the Lord your God for the good land he has given you.]

-3 You're proud of all you have accomplished and think you can achieve anything you want. You forgot ISAIAH 2:22, DON'T TRUST IN YOURSELF. Say verse or go back.

[Stop trusting in man,] who has but a breath in his nostrils. Of what account is he?

9-4 You keep bragging about the great work you did putting the bike together, only to find out the brakes won't work. You forgot MATTHEW 23:12, THE PROUD WILL BE HUMBLED. Say verse or go back.

For [whoever exalts himself will be humbled, and whoever humbles himself will be exalted.

0-1 You are at the park, dying of thirst, and don't have any money. Your friends tell you to just swipe a coke, and you do. You forgot PROVERBS 1:10, DO NOT GIVE IN TO SIN. Say verse or go back.

My son, [if sinners entice you, do not give in to them.]

10-2 You are so tempted to eat the piece of cake your mom is saving. You remember 1 CORINTHIANS 10:13, GOD WILL HELP YOU OVERCOME TEMPTATION. Say verse to move ahead or try for Key Verse.

No temptation has seized you except what is common to man. And [God is faithful; he will not let you be tempted beyond what you can bear.] But when you are tempted, he will also provide a way out so that you can stand up under it.

-3 You need a new bike for your paper route but don't have any money to buy one. You see a bike left by some trees, but you don't take it. You remember HEBREWS 4:16, GOD UNDERSTANDS OUR NEEDS. Say verse to move ahead or try for Key Verse.

et us then approach the throne of grace with nfidence, so that we may receive mercy and find ace to help us in our time of need.]

10-4 You need money and find $20 on the floor of your parents' closet. You keep it, saying, "God must have put it there for me." You forgot JAMES 1:13, GOD DOES NOT TEMPT US. Say verse or go back.

When tempted, no one should say, "God is tempting me." For [God cannot be tempted by evil, nor does he tempt anyone.]

1-1 The other team says it's their turn to go first. You say it's yours and start arguing with them. You forgot PROVERBS 20:3, AVOID AN ARGUMENT. Say verse or go back.

[It is to a man's honor to avoid strife,] but every fool is quick to quarrel.

11-2 Your mom asks you to help with the dishes. You whine that you've already done enough work. You forgot PHILIPPIANS 2:14,15, DO EVERYTHING WITHOUT COMPLAINING OR ARGUING. Say verse or go back.

[Do everything without complaining or arguing,] so that you may become blameless and pure, children of God without fault in a crooked and depraved generation.

1-3 At the parade, the policeman tells you to move. You don't see why you should, but you don't argue. You remember TITUS 3:1,2, DO WHAT IS GOOD. Say verse to move ahead or try for Key Verse.

Remind the people to be subject to rulers and authorities, to be obedient, to [be ready to do whatever is good,] to slander no one, to be peaceable and considerate, and to show true humility toward all men.

11-4 You don't argue with the umpire over a bad call. You remember JAMES 3:17, BE PEACE-LOVING. Say verse to move ahead or try for Key Verse.

But [the wisdom that comes from heaven is first of all pure; then peace-loving,] considerate, submissive, full of mercy and good fruit, impartial and sincere.

2-1 You start telling everyone about the trouble your brother is in. You forgot PROVERBS 17:9, DON'T REPEAT STORIES. Say verse or go back.

He who covers over an offense promotes love, but [whoever repeats the matter separates close friends.]

12-2 You want to tell your sister that you think she is stupid, but you don't. You remember MATTHEW 12:36, BE CAREFUL WHAT YOU SAY. Say verse to move ahead or try for Key Verse.

But I tell you that [men will have to give account on the day of judgment for every careless word they have spoken.]

2-3 Your friend starts criticizing someone you know. You say something nice about the person. You remember EPHESIANS 4:29, BUILD OTHERS UP. Say verse to move ahead or try for Key Verse.

Do not let any unwholesome talk come out of your mouths,] but only what is helpful for building others up according to their needs, that it may benefit those who listen.

12-4 You're whispering bad things about someone you don't like to the other team members. You forgot JAMES 4:11, DON'T SLANDER OTHERS. Say verse or go back.

Brothers, [do not slander one another.] Anyone who speaks against his brother or judges him speaks against the law and judges it.

3-1 You didn't come home when you were supposed to. You made up a good story to keep from getting in trouble. You forgot PROVERBS 12:22, GOD HATES LYING. Say verse or go back.

[The Lord detests lying lips,] but he delights in men who are truthful.

13-2 You told a lie to cover-up what you did wrong. Now you feel terrible and all alone. You forgot ISAIAH 59:2, LYING SEPARATES US FROM GOD. Say verse or go back.

But [your iniquities have separated you from your God;] your sins have hidden his face from you, so that he will not hear.

3-3 When someone tries to convince you that the Bible isn't true, you know that person believes a lie. You remember JOHN 8:44b, SATAN IS THE FATHER OF LIES. Say verse to move ahead or try for Key Verse.

He was a murderer from the beginning, not holding to the truth, for there is no truth in him. When he lies, he speaks his native language, for [he is a liar and the father of lies.]

13-4 You watch a nature program on T.V. They talk about evolution and how there is no God. You remember JEREMIAH 9:6, THE GREATEST LIE IS DENYING GOD. Say verse to move ahead or try for Key Verse.

You live in the midst of deception; [in their deceit they refuse to acknowledge me, declares the Lord.]

4-1 You did some bad things, and you've never asked God for forgiveness. Your prayers aren't being answered. You forgot PROVERBS 15:29, THE WICKED ARE SEPARATED FROM GOD. Say verse or go back.

[The Lord is far from the wicked] but he hears the prayers of the righteous.

14-2 You get in trouble every time you are with a certain group of kids. You shouldn't hang around with them. You forgot ISAIAH 59:7, THE WICKED ARE QUICK TO SIN. Say verse or go back.

[Their feet rush into sin;] they are swift to shed innocent blood. Their thoughts are evil thoughts; ruin and destruction mark their ways.

4-3 A teacher says bad things about Jesus. You know he is in darkness, and what he says can't be trusted. You remember JOHN 3:19, THE WICKED HATE THE LIGHT. Say verse to move ahead or try for Key Verse.

This is the verdict: Light has come into the world, but [men loved darkness instead of light because their deeds were evil.]

5-1 You try to get on the bus by the back door because you don't want to pay. You forgot PROVERBS 20:23, GOD HATES CHEATING. Say verse or go back.

[The Lord detests differing weights,] and dishonest scales do not please him.

5-3 You can't figure out why you've felt so bad ever since you stole that candy bar. You forgot ZECHARIAH 5:3, A THIEF IS SEPARATED FROM GOD. Say verse or go back.

And he said to me, "This is the curse that is going out over the whole land; for according to what it says on one side, [every thief will be banished."]

6-1 At first you thought throwing eggs would be a harmless prank, but then you realize it could hurt people and property. You remember PROVERBS 11:27, ONE WHO SEEKS EVIL FINDS IT. Say verse to move ahead or try for Key Verse.

He who seeks good finds goodwill, but [evil comes to him who searches for it.]

14-4 You meet a self-centered person who only thinks about herself. You remember 2 TIMOTHY 3:2,3, THE WICKED LOVE THEMSELVES INSTEAD OF GOD. Say verse to move ahead or try for Key Verse.

[People will be lovers of themselves,] lovers of money, boastful, proud, abusive, disobedient to their parents, ungrateful, unholy, without love, unforgiving, slanderous, without self-control, brutal, not lovers of the good.

15-2 You were given too much change at the store. You go in to give it back. You remember LEVITICUS 6:4, STEALING IS SIN. Say verse to move ahead or try for Key Verse.

[When he thus sins and becomes guilty, he must return what he has stolen] or taken by extortion, or what was entrusted to him, or the lost property he found.

15-4 You think about cheating on a test you didn't study for but you don't, because you know it is wrong. You remember 1 CORINTHIANS 6:9a, THE EVIL ARE KEPT OUT OF HEAVEN. Say verse to move ahead or try for Key Verse.

[Do you not know that the wicked will not inherit the kingdom of God?]

16-2 You made sure someone else got the blame for something you did bad, but later you were found out. You forgot PSALM 7:15,16 ONE WHO CAUSES TROUBLE WILL GET TROUBLE. Say verse or go back.

[He who digs a hole and scoops it out falls into the pit he has made.] The trouble he causes recoils on himself; his violence comes down on his own head.

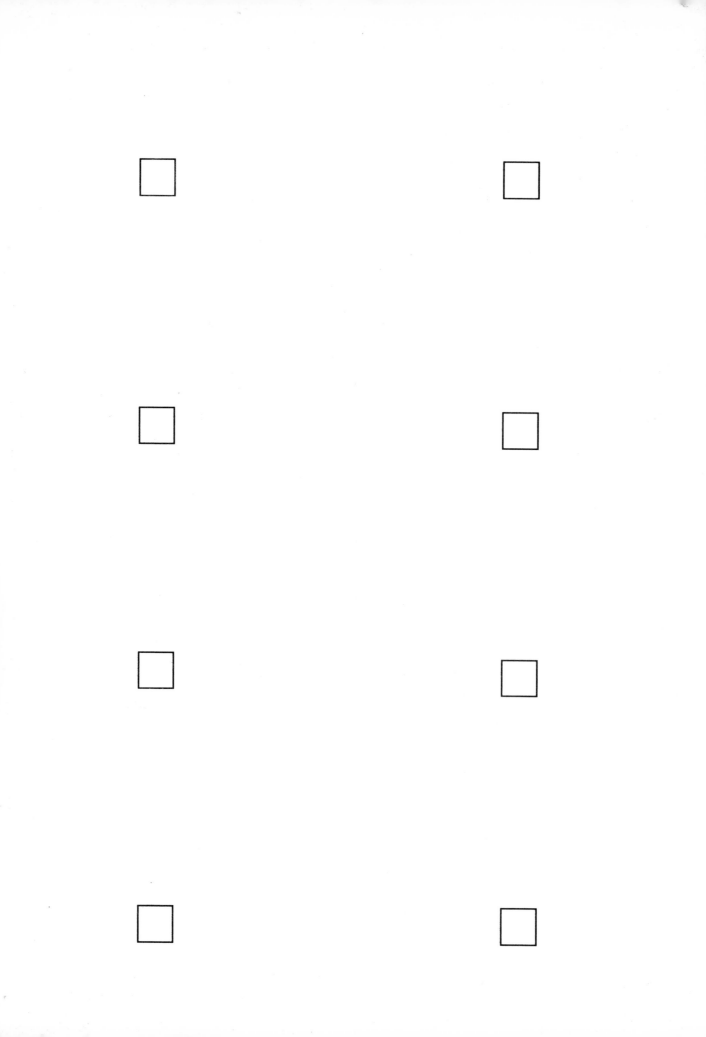

5-3 You really dislike the girl down the street and figure out ways to get other kids to dislike her too. You forgot ZECHARIAH 8:17, DON'T PLOT EVIL. Say verse or go back.

["Do not plot evil against your neighbor,] and do not love to swear falsely. I hate all this," declares the Lord.

16-4 When you realized you were planning to do some bad things, you stopped and prayed for a change of heart. You remember 1 PETER 3:12, GOD IS AGAINST EVIL DOERS. Say verse to move ahead or try for Key Verse.

For the eyes of the Lord are on the righteous and his ears are attentive to their prayer, but [the face of the Lord is against those who do evil.]

7-1 You lay awake at night trying to figure out how to get even with the boy down the street. You forgot LEVITICUS 19:18, DON'T SEEK REVENGE. Say verse or go back.

[Do not seek revenge or bear a grudge against one of your people,] but love your neighbor as yourself. I am the Lord.

17-2 You think there is no way that the boy who stole your lunch is going to get what he deserves unless you take care of him. You forgot PSALM 94:9 GOD KNOWS WHAT IS GOING ON. Say verse or go back.

Does he who implanted the ear not hear? [Does he who formed the eye not see?]

7-3 You could have gotten back at your brother by telling lies and getting him in trouble too, but you knew that wouldn't please God. You remember ROMANS 12:17, DON'T PAY BACK EVIL. Say verse to move ahead or try for Key Verse.

[Do not repay anyone evil for evil.] Be careful to do what is right in the eyes of everybody.

17-4 Some people have been saying some really mean things about you, but you ignore them. You remember 1 PETER 2:23, DON'T MAKE THREATS. Say verse to move ahead or try for Key Verse.

When they hurled their insults at him, he did not retaliate; [when he suffered, he made no threats.]

18-1 You have lots of toys but wouldn't give any to the Christmas box to help other children. You forgot PROVERBS 14:31, BE KIND. Say verse or go back.

He who oppresses the poor shows contempt for their Maker, but [whoever is kind to the needy honors God.]

18-2 The other kids are teasing a kid unfairly. You defend him even though you know they'll turn on you. You remember MICAH 6:8, LOVE MERCY. Say verse to move ahead or try for Key Verse.

He has shown you, O man, what is good. And [what does the Lord require of you? To act justly and to love mercy] and to walk humbly with your God.

8-3 Even though you sometimes get discouraged trying to do things God's way when no one else seems to want to, you stay on His path. You remember GALATIANS 6:9, DO GOOD. Say verse to move ahead or try for Key Verse.

[Let us not become weary in doing good,] for at the proper time we will reap a harvest if we do not give up.

18-4 You make fun of the kids down the street who don't have new clothes. You forgot COLOSSIANS 3:12, BE COMPASSIONATE. Say verse or go back.

Therefore as God's chosen people, holy and dearly loved, [clothe yourselves with compassion,] kindness, humility, gentleness, and patience.

9-1 You gave all the money you were saving for a baseball glove to help out the family who didn't have any money for food. You feel so close to God. You remember PROVERBS 11:25, REFRESH OTHERS. Say verse to move ahead or try for Key Verse.

A generous man will prosper; [he who refreshes others will himself be refreshed.]

19-2 Your family decides not to go out to eat anymore so you can give all the money you save for famine relief. You remember ISAIAH 58:10, SATISFY THE NEEDS OF OTHERS. Say verse to move ahead or try for Key Verse.

If you spend yourselves in behalf of the hungry and [satisfy the needs of the oppressed,] then your light will rise in the darkness, and your night will become like the noonday.

19-3 Your mom asks if she can buy you cheaper shoes so she can use the money to help the family next door whose father is out of a job. You want the expensive shoes. You forgot MATTHEW 25:40, GIVE AS TO JESUS. Say verse or go back.

The King will reply, "I tell you the truth, [whatever you did for one of the least of these brothers of mine, you did for me."]

19-4 You didn't think of anyone else on their birthdays. On your birthday no one gives you anything. You forgot 2 CORINTHIANS 9:6, BE GENEROUS. Say verse or go back.

Remember this: Whoever sows sparingly will also reap sparingly, and [whoever sows generously will also reap generously.]

20-1 You keep talking about needing money to go to camp. Your mom says she has jobs for you to do, but you don't want to do them. You don't have enough money to go. You forgot PROVERBS 14:23, WORK HARD. Say verse or go back.

[All hard work brings a profit,] but mere talk leads only to poverty.

20-2 Your father tells you to clean up the garage, but you spend the whole day messing around. At dinner time you still have work to do. You forgot PROVERBS 19:15, DON'T BE LAZY. Say verse or go back.

Laziness brings on deep sleep, and [the shiftless man goes hungry.]

0-3   When you have a job to do, you always try to do your very best work. You remember ECCLESIASTES 11:6, WORK TO SUCCEED. Say verse to move ahead or try for Key Verse.

[Sow your seed in the morning, and at evening let not your hands be idle,] for you do not know which will succeed, whether this or that, or whether both will do equally well.

20-4   You see how hard your dad is working and ask how you can help him out. Your dad knows how important it is to work. You remember 2 THESSALONIANS 3:10, KEEP BUSY. Say verse to move ahead or try for Key Verse.

For even when we were with you we gave you this rule: ["If a man will not work, he shall not eat."]

KEY VERSE REFERENCE SHEET

Use this sheet to give Bible reference and topic when a player wants to recite a Key Verse. Store this with the game board.

1 DEFINING WISDOM   PROVERBS 9:10
The fear of the Lord is the beginning of wisdom, and knowledge of the Holy
One is understanding.

2 BECOMING WISE   PROVERBS 4:1
Listen, my sons, to a father's instruction; pay attention and gain understanding.

3 RECOGNIZING THE WISE MAN   PROVERBS 14:16
A wise man fears the Lord and shuns evil, but a fool is hotheaded and reckless.

4 STAYING AWAY FROM THE FOOLISH MAN   PROVERBS 10:23
A fool finds pleasure in evil conduct, but a man of understanding delights in
wisdom.

5 CHOOSING YOUR FRIENDS   2 CORINTHIANS 6:15
What harmony is there between Christ and Belial? What does a believer have
in common with an unbeliever?

6 BEING A FRIEND   PROVERBS 17:17
A friend loves at all times, and a brother is born for adversity.

7 HONORING YOUR PARENTS   PROVERBS 30:17
The eye that mocks a father, that scorns obedience to a mother, will be pecked
out by the ravens of the valley, will be eaten by the vultures.

8 CONTROLLING YOUR ANGER   PROVERBS 15:1
A gentle answer turns away wrath, but a harsh word stirs up anger.

9 GIVING UP YOUR PRIDE   ISAIAH 2:11
The eyes of the arrogant man will be humbled and the pride of men brought
low; the Lord alone will be exalted in that day.

10 OVERCOMING TEMPTATION   HEBREWS 4:15
For we do not have a high priest who is unable to sympathize with our
weaknesses, but we have one who was tempted in every way, just as we are -
yet without sin.

11 ARGUING AND COMPLAINING   PROVERBS 18:6
A fool's lips bring him strife, and his mouth invites a beating.

12 GOSSIPING   EXODUS 23:1
Do not spread false reports. Do not help a wicked man by being a malicious witness.

13 LYING   PROVERBS 13:3
He who guards his lips guards his life, but he who speaks rashly will come to ruin.

14 BEING WICKED   PSALM 9:16
The Lord is known by his justice; the wicked are ensnared by the work of their hands.

15 CHEATING AND STEALING   PROVERBS 28:6
Better a poor man whose walk is blameless than a rich man whose ways are perverse.

16 PLOTTING EVIL   PROVERBS 14:22
Do not those who plot evil go astray? But those who plan what is good find love and faithfulness.

17 SEEKING REVENGE   PROVERBS 20:22
Do not say, "I'll pay you back for this wrong!" Wait for the Lord, and he will deliver you.

18 SHOWING GOODNESS AND MERCY   PROVERBS 3:27
Do not withhold good from those who deserve it when it is in your power to act.

19 GIVING AND BEING GENEROUS   LUKE 6:38
Give, and it will be given to you. A good measure, pressed down, shaken together and running over, will be poured into your lap. For with the measure you use, it will be measured to you.

20 WORKING HARD   PROVERBS 28:19
He who works his land will have abundant food, but the one who chases fantasies will have his fill of poverty.

TREASURE SHEET

Make copies of this sheet, then cut the copies apart on the dotted line. Give a small Treasure Sheet to each player to fill up by reciting Key Verses. Always keep the original to make more copies as needed.

2	3	4	5		1	2	3	4	5
7	8	9	10		6	7	8	9	10
1	12	13	14	15	11	12	13	14	15
6	17	18	19	20	16	17	18	19	20

2	3	4	5		1	2	3	4	5
7	8	9	10		6	7	8	9	10
1	12	13	14	15	11	12	13	14	15
6	17	18	19	20	16	17	18	19	20

2	3	4	5		1	2	3	4	5
7	8	9	10		6	7	8	9	10
11	12	13	14	15	11	12	13	14	15
16	17	18	19	20	16	17	18	19	20